ORIGAMI
OCEAN FRIENDS

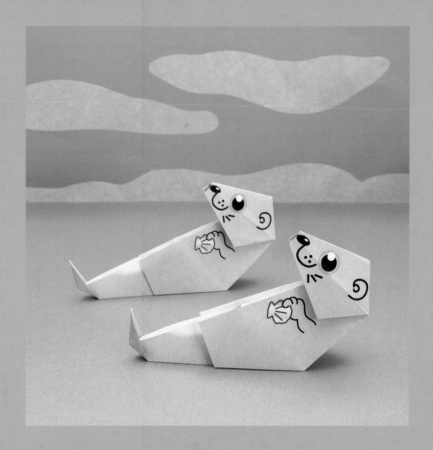

ORIGAMI OCEAN FRIENDS

35 water-based favorites to fold in an instant

MARI ONO

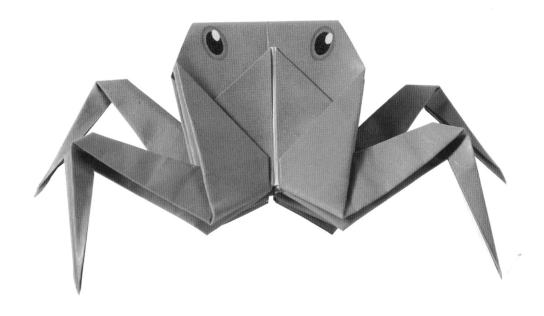

CICO BOOKS

LONDON NEW YORK

Published in 2018 by CICO Books
An imprint of Ryland Peters & Small Ltd
20–21 Jockey's Fields   341 E 116th St
London WC1R 4BW   New York, NY 10029

www.rylandpeters.com

10 9 8 7 6 5 4 3 2

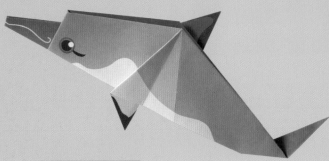

MIX
Paper from
responsible sources
FSC® C106563
FSC
www.fsc.org

Text © Mari Ono 2018
Design, illustration,
and photography © CICO Books 2018

A CIP catalog record for this book is available from the
Library of Congress and the British Library.

ISBN: 978 1 78249 637 3

Printed in China

Editor: Robin Gurdon
Designer: Jerry Goldie
Photographer: Geoff Dann
Paper illustration: Takumasa Ono
Photography styling and set design: Nel Haynes

THANKS

First and foremost, I would like to thank the readers for purchasing this
book. It could not have been put together without the generous help
and cooperation of "my origami book team:" Robin Gurdon, Geoff Dann,
and my husband, Takumasa. It's now over 12 years that we have been
working together as a team!

Working with Robin and Geoff is always a pleasure. On all my books
Robin has always put 100 percent effort into correcting my English
text and making notes on the origami steps during the shoots. Similarly,
Geoff also ensures things run smoothly, giving me simple directions
when shooting and always delivering great photos for the readers. The
completion of the book would not have been possible if these two were
not around and the partnership between author, photographer, and
editor is always cherished.

Designing the origami papers takes a long time due to the process
of working out how the illustration will fit on the finished papers. My
husband, Takumasa, has always undertaken this complicated job and,
again, without his help all the origami models would not look so
impressive.

CONTENTS

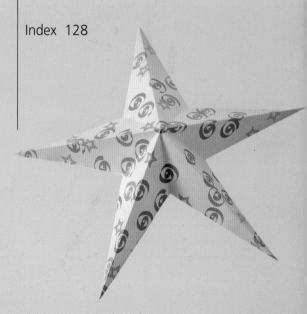

INTRODUCTION

Communication between parents and children is crucial to help a child to develop its cognitive ability, but in recent years this relationship has been affected by the growth of technology and the rise of the Internet.

Nowadays, when children have a question, they often turn to the Internet for an answer, rather than asking an adult. Also, children are spending less time with their friends, because their idea of "fun" is to spend time online. With the Internet becoming a substitute for physical interaction between people, some children are having difficulties communicating with and understanding others, and expressing themselves clearly.

In order to encourage communication between a parent and child, it is important for families to spend time together. They should not only sit and talk with each other, but also take part in fun activities together. This way the children will acquire new skills and knowledge through natural interaction.

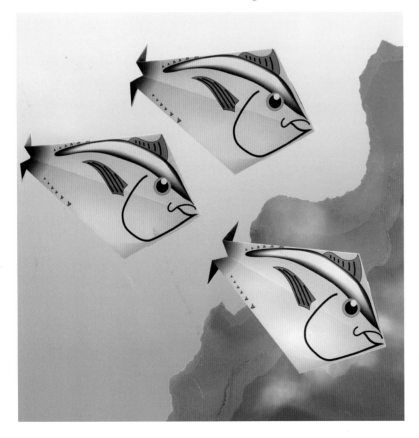

In Japan, parent-child communication is encouraged through creative activities. One of the most popular activities is origami play, which has been delighting Japanese kids since the eighteenth century. The skills needed to make origami models have been passed down through the generations, with grandparents, parents, brothers, sisters, and friends all sharing with children the secrets of this fun craft.

Not only is origami is a great hobby, but it also has educational benefits. Playing with origami in early childhood education helps to develop concentration and a child's cerebrum, cultivating a creative and imaginative mind. Kids progress quicker when they are having fun.

In addition to the benefits to early years development, origami will also increase opportunities for parent-child communication. It may be considered a child's hobby, but adults enjoy origami as well, and by making models together a connection is formed. Teamwork and guidance from both parties will enhance creative thinking and strengthen bonds. And of course, making a 3D model from 2D paper is pretty cool!

This book introduces 35 origami models inspired by our ocean friends. Some of the models are easy to make; others are a bit more difficult, even for parents. Over the years of making and teaching origami I have heard many adults say, "I don't do origami because it's quite tricky," but after making one model many find that the challenge is very rewarding. For a parent to learn the basic steps of origami and then teach them to a child can also develop the parent's own cognitive skills, concentration, and patience. Moreover, parents can become a creative role model. However, this book is not just for parents to learn the steps and teach their child. It is designed so that both grown-ups and kids can enjoy each other's company while developing both cognitive and dexterity skills, as well as stimulating an imaginative mind.

After mastering a few basic origami folds, anyone can make anything, and that is why origami has been around for nearly 300 years. I hope that origami play can be used as a tool for communication between all the members of the family. Let's not think that origami is difficult, let's think of it is a creative challenge that's lots of fun, which also helps people to build new skills and bonds. Enjoy!

PART ONE

ALONG THE COASTLINE

1 KAMOME | SEAGULL

The seagull inhabits almost all the world's seas, flying over every part of the ocean as well as almost any inland stretch of water you can find. Making this origami seagull is very easy and a good tip for making it especially realistic is to round both wings into an arch shape so that the bird looks like it's gliding across the water.

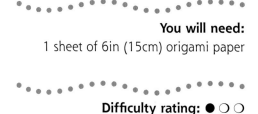

You will need:
1 sheet of 6in (15cm) origami paper

Difficulty rating: ● ○ ○

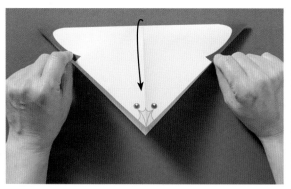

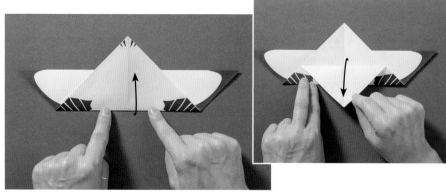

1 Fold the paper in half from corner to corner through the design to make a crease and open out. Next fold the paper in half between the remaining corners.

2 Fold up the bottom point using the marks on the paper as a guide, then fold back the upper sheet of the new flap, again using the marks on the paper to guide you.

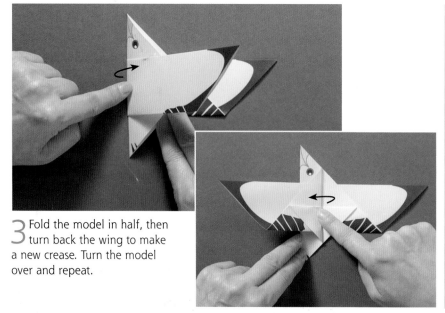

3 Fold the model in half, then turn back the wing to make a new crease. Turn the model over and repeat.

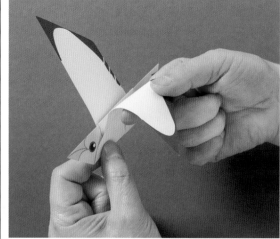

4 Pick up the model and curl the flaps over your fingers to make the shape of a wing in flight.

OCEAN INSIGHT

Gulls can be found across all continents of the world and not just by the sea. Many can now be seen in cities and towns, too.

2 SHIROKUMA | POLAR BEAR

You will need:
2 sheets of 6in (15cm) origami paper
Paper glue

Difficulty rating: ● ○ ○

Polar bears spend their lives fighting the cold weather of Arctic, swimming vast distances in the freezing water to find their food. Though they seem tough, this origami shows their adorable side. Try drawing your own style of face onto the model to make a unique polar bear.

1 Take the sheet for the body and, with the design side down, fold it in half from corner to corner both ways, opening out each time, to make creases. Then fold the top and bottom points over to meet in the center of the paper.

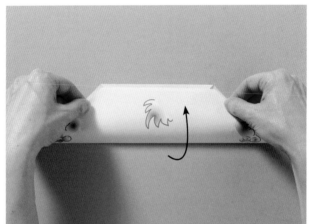

2 Fold the paper in half along the central crease.

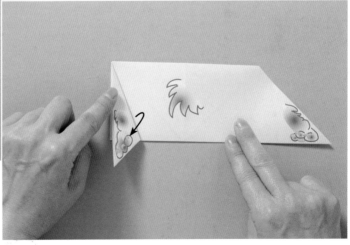

3 Fold in the bottom left corner, ensuring the bottom edge is straight. Next fold back the new flap so that the diagonal crease now runs down the vertical edges. Repeat on the right-hand side.

4 Turn the paper over and fold over the top two corners, using the marks on the paper as a guide.

5 Take the second sheet of paper and fold it in half from corner to corner across the design, then fold up the outer corners to meet at the top point.

6 Fold back the newly made flaps, making an angled fold along the line marked on the design, then fold back the tips, ensuring the outer edges align.

OCEAN INSIGHT

Polar bears may have white fur, but their skin is black. This helps them to absorb heat from the sun and stay warm in Arctic conditions.

7 Fold in the bottom corners of the flaps using the marks on the paper as a guide, then fold in the protruding corners above over the edges of the flaps.

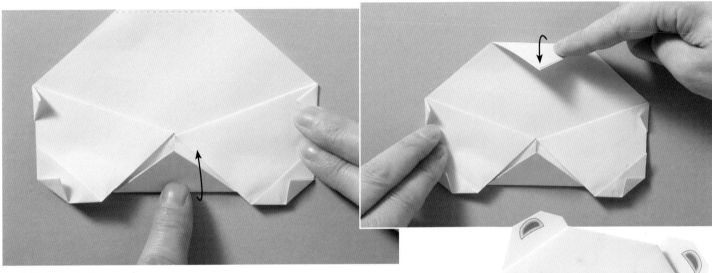

8 Fold in the bottom and top points, again using the marks printed on the design as a guide.

9 Stick the two sheets of paper together using paper glue.

3 LACK CO | SEA OTTER

Sea otters are fascinating creatures. They live most of the time in the sea, staying within sight of the coast, and when they go to sleep while in the water they cling onto seaweed to stop them drifting out to sea. The sea otter's face will look best if the crease that makes its jaw is firmly pressed right along the dotted line marked on the design.

You will need:
1 sheet of 6in (15cm) origami paper

Difficulty rating: ● ○ ○

1 Fold the paper in half from corner to corner through the design to make a crease and open up. Fold the right-hand edges in to meet along the central crease, then fold in the left-hand edges in the same way.

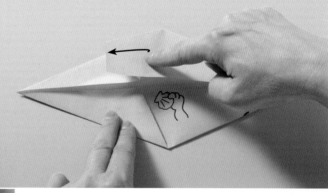

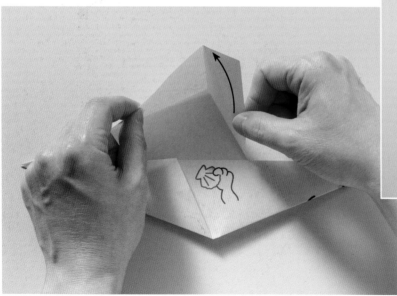

2 Open up the flaps on the top side of the model then fold them back down, this time with the right-hand side on top of the left, reversing the direction of some of the creases, as shown in the photograph.

ALONG THE COASTLINE

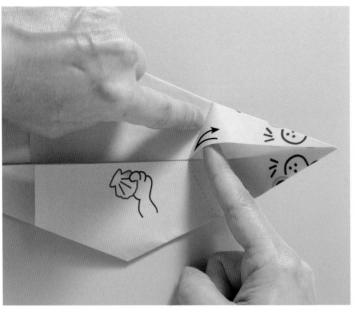

3 Carefully make a diagonal crease across the top layer on each side, along the lines marked on the design.

4 In preparation of forming the shape of the otter, pull up the right-hand point of the model, opening the gap between the edges of the paper.

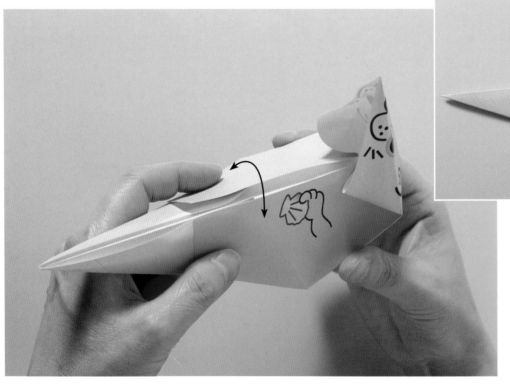

5 Lift the paper off the table and carefully fold the model in half along its length, allowing the head to form around the body before flattening it into position.

6 Turn the end of the nose back to make a crease, then open up the model and fold it back inside to form the snout.

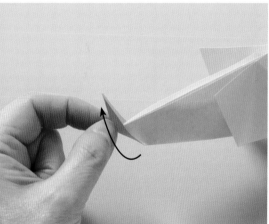

7 In the same way, fold over the point at the other end of the model to make a crease and fold this inside as well to create the tail.

OCEAN INSIGHT

The fur of the sea otter is the densest of all animals. Just 1 square inch (2.5cm²) of their body can be covered with up to 1 million hairs.

4 AZARASHI | SEAL

Like their cousins the sea lions, seals are mammals that live around the coasts of many of the world's seas. Since they appear frequently in both aquariums and fairy tales, they are one of the most well-known and popular of all the ocean creatures. This model is made using just the most basic techniques, so have fun mastering them!

You will need:
1 sheet of 6in (15cm) origami paper

Difficulty rating: ● ○ ○

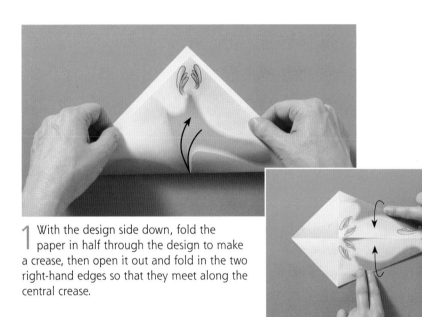

1 With the design side down, fold the paper in half through the design to make a crease, then open it out and fold in the two right-hand edges so that they meet along the central crease.

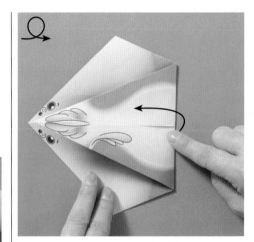

2 Turn the paper over and fold over the right-hand point so that it sits on the left-hand point.

3 Turn the paper back over and pick up the corner of the upper flap sitting on the central crease. Take it over to the right so that the edge of the flap runs along the central crease. Repeat on the bottom flap.

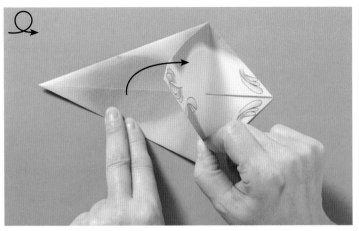

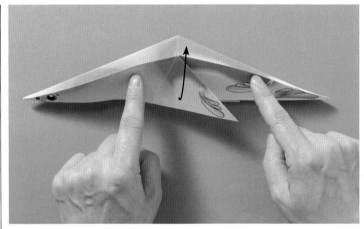

4 Turn the paper back over again and fold the upper flap from the left over to the right to form a long diamond.

5 Fold the model in half along its length.

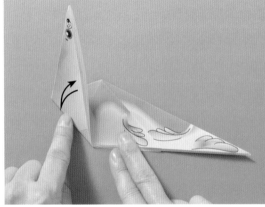

6 Fold up the left-hand point at an angle to make a crease, then form a second angled crease in the opposite direction.

7 Lift up the model and open up the body, refolding the left-hand point inside to form the neck of the seal, reversing the direction of the folds where necessary, then press flat.

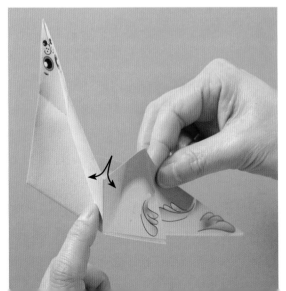

8 Repeat at the second crease to form the seal's head.

9 Turn back the end point to form a vertical crease, then open up the head and refold the tip inside to form the snout.

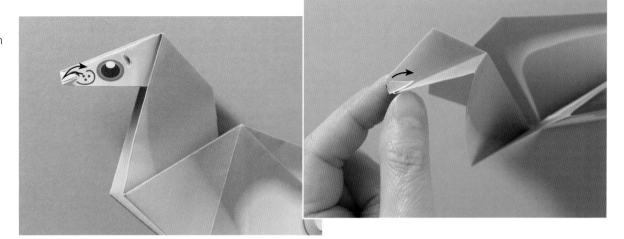

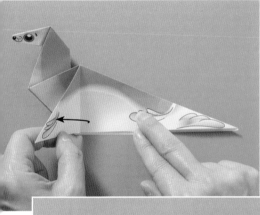

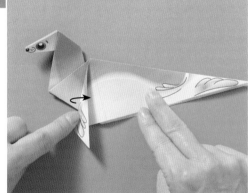

10 With the paper back on the table turn the triangular flap forward then fold it in half by running the diagonal edge down the vertical crease. Turn over and repeat on the other side.

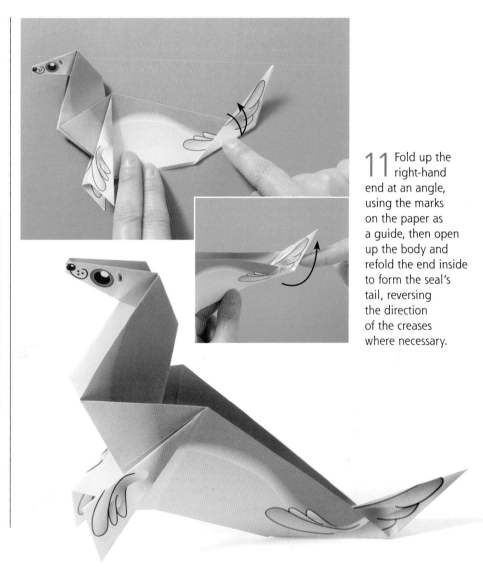

11 Fold up the right-hand end at an angle, using the marks on the paper as a guide, then open up the body and refold the end inside to form the seal's tail, reversing the direction of the creases where necessary.

5 TSUNOMEDORI | PUFFIN

Did you know that puffins primarily live in the North Atlantic and Arctic Oceans, flying huge distances from their cliff-top nests to search for food? This origami emphasizes the vibrant colors for which puffins are so famous. Make sure to fold each step firmly to achieve a perfect, pointy beak.

You will need:
1 sheet of 6in (15cm) origami paper

Difficulty rating: ● ● ○

1 With the printed side face down, fold the paper in half through the design to make a crease and open out, then fold the two lower edges in so that they meet along the central crease.

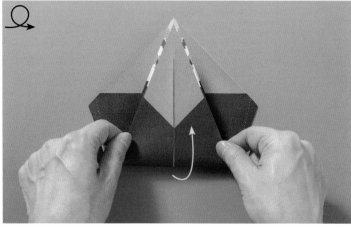

2 Turn the paper over and fold up the bottom point to the top.

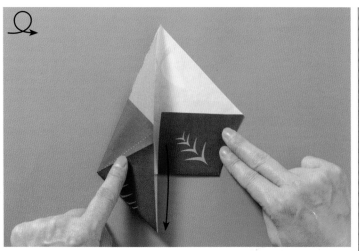

3 Turn the paper back over and pick up the corner of the flap sitting on the central crease and fold it downward so that the entire edge of the flap runs down the center. Repeat on the other flap.

4 Lift the top flap and press down a diagonal crease across its left-hand side using the marks on the design as a guide, taking care just to press from the edge to the central crease. Close it back down and repeat on the right-hand side of the same flap.

OCEAN INSIGHT
Puffins develop their distinctive colorful beaks only during the spring breeding season, which helps them to attract mates. They then shed this distinctive beak later on in the year.

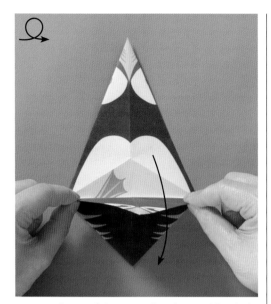

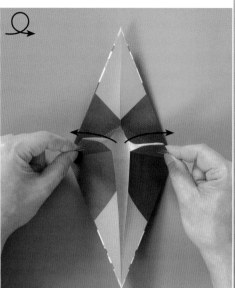

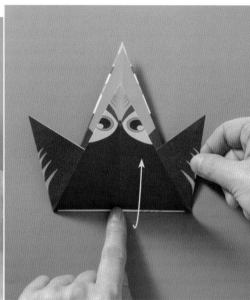

5 Turn the model over and make two identical diagonal creases on this side then fold back the entire flap to the bottom using the horizontal crease.

6 Turn the paper over again and lift the two triangular flaps, pulling them gently outward. As the top and bottom points are pulled together flatten the model using the creases made in the previous steps.

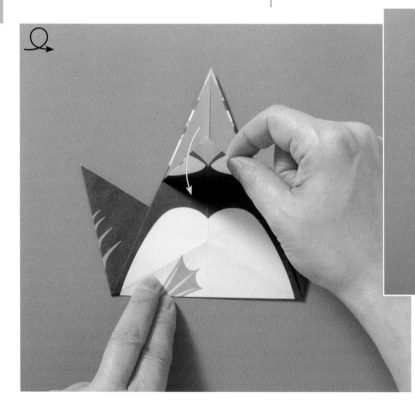

7 Turn the model over. Fold down the tip of the upper flap to the bottom edge of the model then turn the tip over to the right to make a crease, ensuring that the edge of the flap runs along the fold line below. Repeat by folding the tip of the flap to the left.

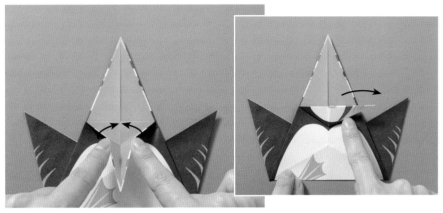

8 Press down the outer parts of the flap so that the edges again run across the model but this time the point of the paper is doubled and stands tall. Fold this tip over to the right.

9 Fold the top point over to the left to make a crease so that the right-hand edge runs horizontally along the edge of the flap just made.

10 As before, make an identical crease on the left then lift the flap and press the two sides together so that the point stands up; fold this to the right.

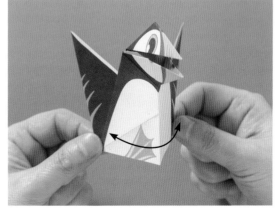

11 Lift up the model and carefully fold it in half along its length, allowing the beak to stand proud.

6 PERIKAN | PELICAN

Pelicans are large but extremely agile birds that dive into the sea from a great height to catch fish, which they then store in their huge, pouch-like beaks. This model is quite intricate but by making the beak three-dimensional, it really looks like this origami pelican has successfully caught tonnes of fish.

You will need:
1 sheet of 6in (15cm) origami paper

Difficulty rating: ● ● ●

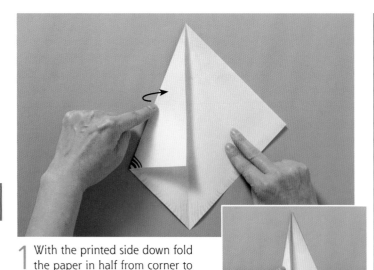

1 With the printed side down fold the paper in half from corner to corner through the design to make a crease. Open it out and fold in the upper edges so that they meet along the central crease, then fold the upper edges in again.

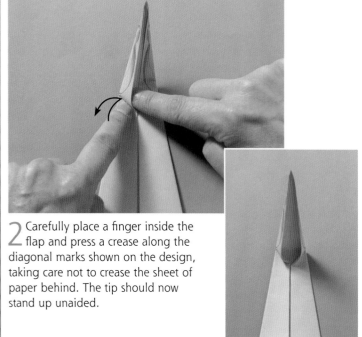

2 Carefully place a finger inside the flap and press a crease along the diagonal marks shown on the design, taking care not to crease the sheet of paper behind. The tip should now stand up unaided.

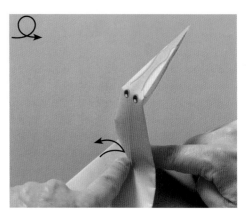

3 Turn the model over and make creases across the body of the model using the marks provided.

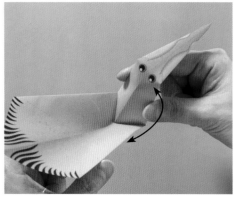

4 Begin to close up the model, reversing the direction of the crease along the neck so that the head is formed in the opposite direction to the body.

OCEAN INSIGHT

A pelican's stretchy beak can hold more than its stomach—with some pelicans able to fit more than 2 ½ gallons (10 liters) of water in there.

5 Make diagonal creases across the tail along the marks shown on the design, then press the body fully shut to form the final model.

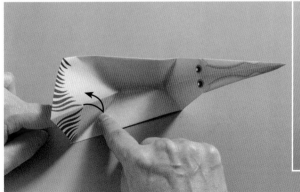

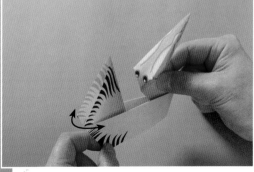

7 PENGIN | PENGUIN

Penguins live mainly around the icy waters of Antarctica. There are many different species but all have adapted to swimming in the sea instead of flying in the sky, using their wings as fins while hunting fish underwater. This origami can be a bit tricky but it is a unique chance to make a parent and child together, so do have a go.

You will need:
1 sheet of 6in (15cm) origami paper

Difficulty rating: ● ● ●

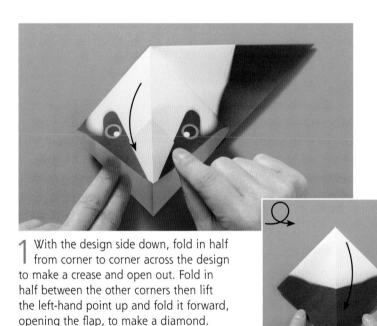

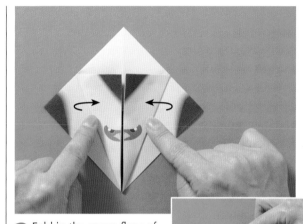

1 With the design side down, fold in half from corner to corner across the design to make a crease and open out. Fold in half between the other corners then lift the left-hand point up and fold it forward, opening the flap, to make a diamond. Turn the paper over and repeat.

2 Fold in the upper flaps of the outer corners so that the lower edges run together along the central crease. Fold the top point forward over the edges of the flaps to make a crease.

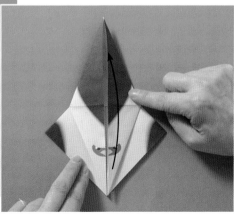

3 Open out the two flaps just made and lift the top sheet of paper, turning the point over the top of the paper to form a long diamond shape. Reverse the direction of the creases where necessary.

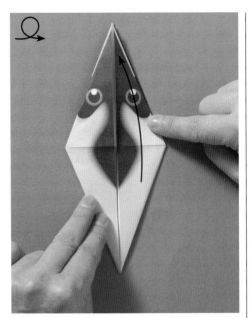

4 Turn the paper over and repeat on the other side.

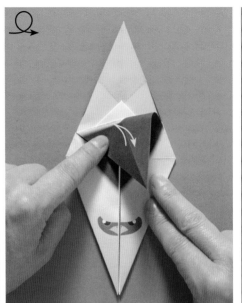

5 Turn the paper back over and fold back the top flap to make a diagonal crease from the left of the central crease along the marked line printed on the design. Release the flap and repeat on the right-hand side of the central crease.

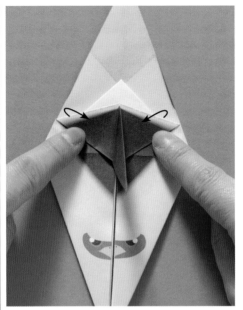

6 Push the sides of the upper flap flat using the pair of creases just made so that the two sides around the point of the flap fold together and stand proud.

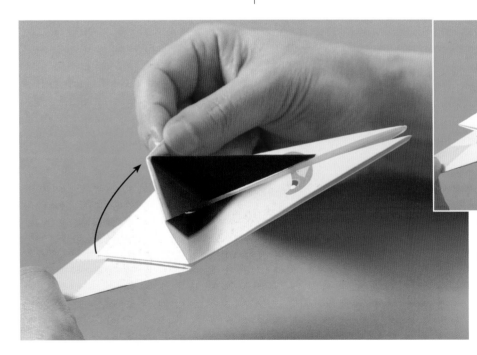

7 Lift the model up and carefully fold forward the tip of the flap so that it passes through the gap between the lower flaps.

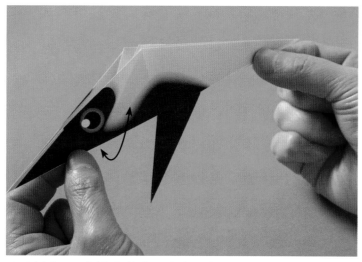

8 Fold the model in half along its length.

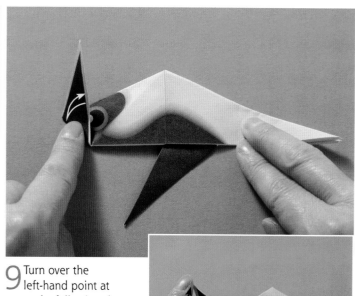

9 Turn over the left-hand point at an angle, following the marks on the paper, then open up the body and fold the tip inside to form the beak, reversing the direction of the creases where necessary.

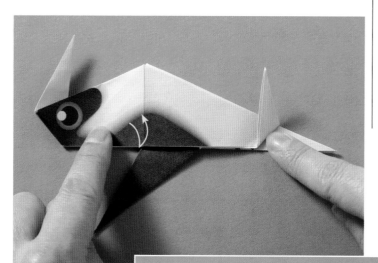

10 Repeat on both tips at the right-hand end of the model to form the bird's feet.

PART TWO

IN THE ROCK POOL

8 KURAGE | JELLYFISH

Though the jellyfish floats in the water like a harmless parachute, it can sting you with the poison held in its long tentacles, which hang below it in the water. The tentacles and body of this origami model are made separately. Both are very simple, so go ahead and make a jellyfish!

You will need:
2 sheets of 6in (15cm) origami paper
Paper glue

Difficulty rating: ● ○ ○

IN THE ROCK POOL

1 Use the first sheet to make the tentacles. With the design side down, fold it in half from side to side, then in half again. Lift the flap, open it, and press it forward to form a triangle. Turn the paper over and repeat.

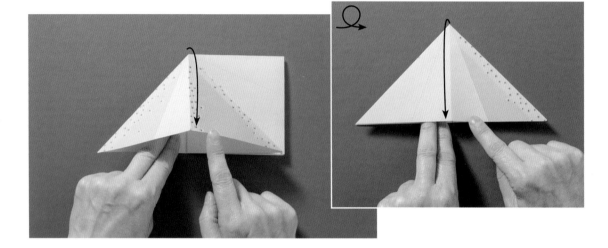

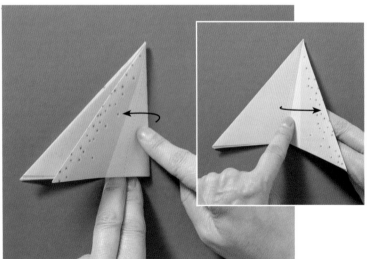

2 Fold the paper in half from right to left then turn back the top flap, using the first set of marks printed on the paper as a guide.

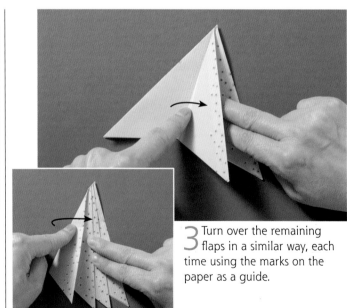

3 Turn over the remaining flaps in a similar way, each time using the marks on the paper as a guide.

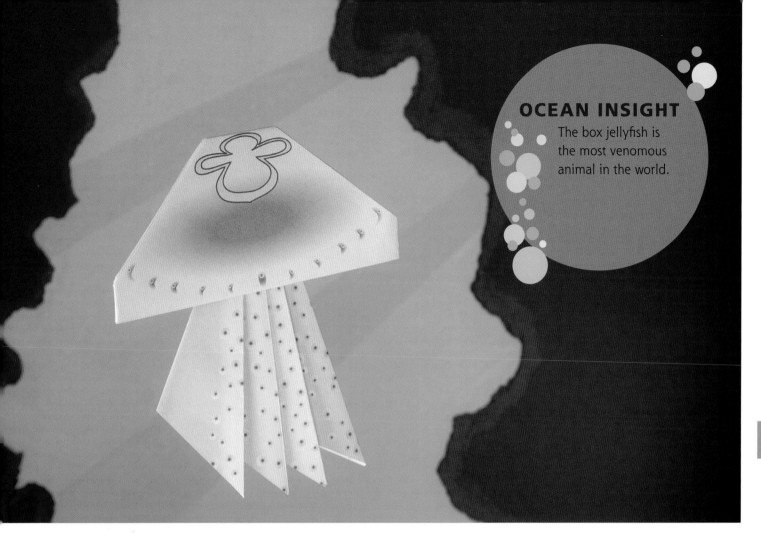

OCEAN INSIGHT

The box jellyfish is the most venomous animal in the world.

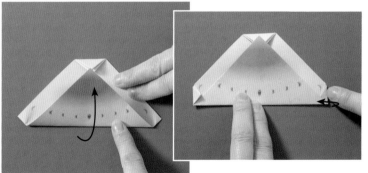

4 Take the second sheet and fold it in half from corner to corner, then fold the outer corners up to meet at the top. Fold down the top point, using the marks on the paper as a guide.

5 Fold up the bottom point, making a crease just below the line of the outer points, as shown by the marks on the paper. Then turn in the side points to make short vertical edges. Finally join the two pieces of paper together using paper glue.

OCEAN INSIGHT

Shells are made mostly from calcium carbonate, a material that has many uses, including as a building material, in medicine to help indigestion, and even in toothpaste.

9 MAKIGAI | SHELLS

There are many different ways in which sea creatures protect themselves and some even create their very own secure habitat to help them survive. The most common form of this is the shell. You can easily make beautiful origami shells as long as you take care to follow the fold lines marked on the design and make sure every crease is crisp.

You will need:
1 sheet of 6in (15cm) origami paper

Difficulty rating: ● ○ ○

1 With the design side face up, fold the paper in half from corner to corner across the design to make a crease, then open out. Fold the bottom right edge over to sit on the top left edge then fold the paper in half again.

2 Fold the uppermost flap across to the left-hand point to make a vertical crease down the center of the paper then open out again.

3 Fold the same point back into the center to make a second crease, opening out again, then fold the point over to the last crease.

4 Turn over the top flap to the right using the central crease.

5 Fold the tip of the next flap on the left over to the center then turn the whole flap over to the right.

6 On the next flap turn the point over to the center, then fold the flap in half again before turning the whole flap over to the right.

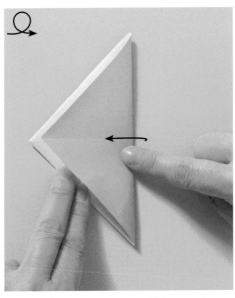

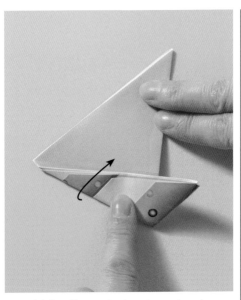

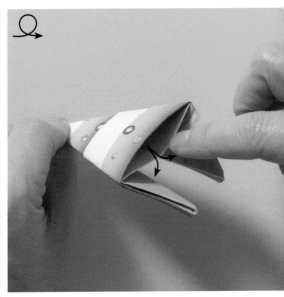

7 Turn the paper over and fold the right-hand point over to the left.

8 Fold the diagonal edges in so that they meet along the central horizontal crease.

9 Lift up the model and turn it over, then carefully open up the pocket beneath the central section of the model.

10 Fold the points into this pocket and press the new creases flat.

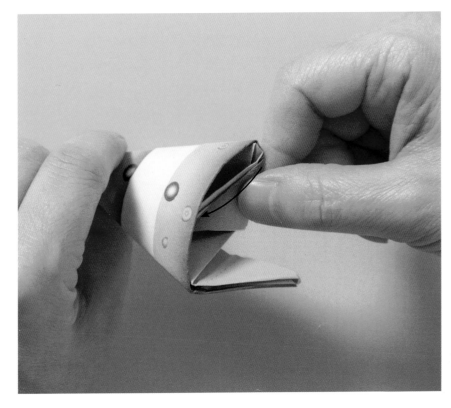

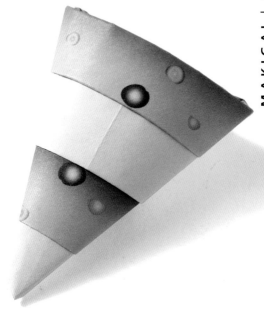

10 SANMA | SKIPPER PIKE

Skipper pike, also known as Pacific saury, swim in vast shoals through the seas and in Japan their presence is seen as a sign of the fall. A skipper pike's silver body looks very sleek under the surface and has often been compared to a sword blade shooting through water. To achieve the closest representation make sure your folds are crisp so that it looks thin and sharp.

You will need:
1 sheet of 6in (15cm) origami paper
Scissors

Difficulty rating: ● ○ ○

OCEAN INSIGHT

Sanma translates as "autumn sword fish" in Japanese. In the fall, *sanma* are found around the Japanese coast and a freshly caught fish can be held upright like a sword thanks to its firm flesh.

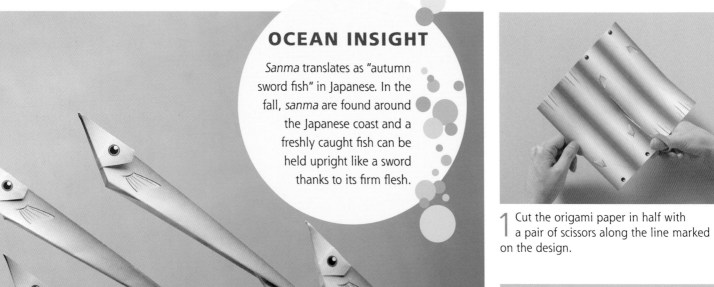

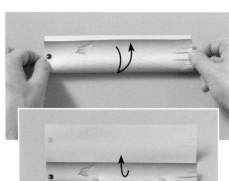

1 Cut the origami paper in half with a pair of scissors along the line marked on the design.

2 Fold one half of the paper in half along its length to make a crease and open out, then fold both long edges in to meet along the central crease.

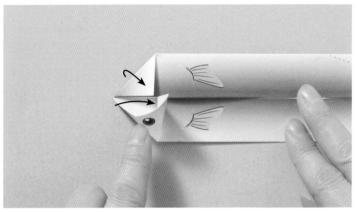

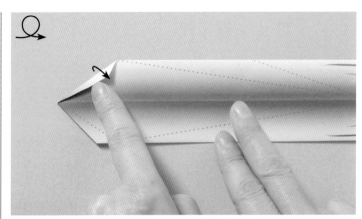

3 Fold over the two corners at the left-hand end. Next open out the flaps and take the corner of paper from inside, refolding it to the right.

4 Turn the paper over and fold in the left-hand edges using the marks on the paper as a guide.

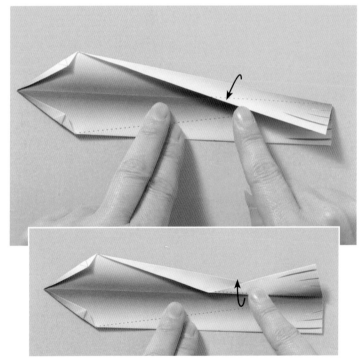

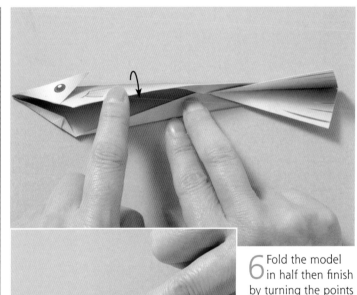

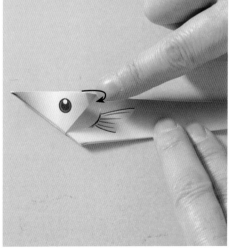

5 Turn over the long edges, making a diagonal fold from the middle of the right-hand edge to the end of the flaps just made, using the marks printed on the design as a guide. Now turn over the corners of these new flaps so that the folds run along the central crease.

6 Fold the model in half then finish by turning the points at the back of the head underneath themselves. Repeat with the other half of the paper to make a second fish.

11 HITODE | STARFISH

As its name implies, the starfish is a five-pronged creature which lives on the seabed and around the coast. Having five arms, it crawls and moves along the ocean floor, however it also frequently appears in rock pools and on the beach. This origami model is based on the mathematical technique of making a square paper into a pentagon.

You will need:
1 sheet of 6in (15cm) origami paper
Scissors

Difficulty rating: ● ● ○

IN THE ROCK POOL

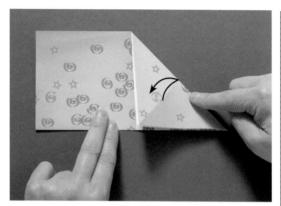

1 With the design face down, fold the bottom edge up to the top then turn the right-hand edge over twice so that it runs first along the top edge, then the bottom, making two diagonal creases.

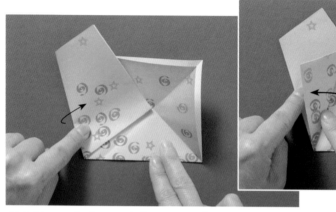

2 Fold over the bottom left corner so that it sits exactly on the crossing point of the two diagonal crease lines made in the first step. Fold this new flap in half by turning the point on the crossing point back to the left-hand edge.

3 Fold over the right-hand edge so that it runs along the right side of the flap made in the last step.

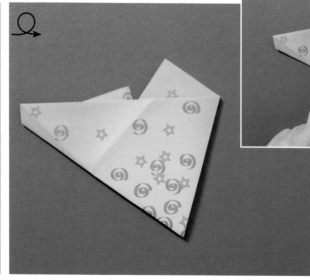

4 Turn the paper over then fold over the right-hand edge so that it sits on the left-hand crease.

OCEAN INSIGHT

Starfish do not have any blood and instead use seawater to pump nutrients through their bodies. They are also able to regrow a limb if a hungry predator decides to take a bite out of one.

5 Use a pair of scissors to cut along the dotted line marked on the design. Discard the larger piece and open up the smaller one, gently creating the shape of the star by reversing the direction of some of the creases so that all the fold lines leading to the points form ridges.

OCEAN INSIGHT
You can find over 1,000 different species of sea anemone at the bottom of oceans and rock pools all over the world.

12 ISOGINTYAKU | SEA ANEMONE

The sea anemone is one of the wondrous creatures of the oceans. Spectacularly colored, they nestle themselves on rocks in the ocean, letting their tendrils waft in the current to collect food. Eight identical, connected pieces make up this origami model, which can then be displayed either way up to show an anemone either feeding or at rest.

· ·

You will need:
2 sheets of 6in (15cm) origami paper
Scissors
Paper glue

Difficulty rating:
● ● ○

1 Cut both sheets of paper into quarters so that you have eight identical pieces of paper.

2 Take one of the squares and fold it in half through the design to make a crease. Open it out and fold the two left-hand edges over so that they meet in the center, then turn the right-hand point over the edges of these flaps to form a crease.

3 Open out the paper and fold over the left-hand corner so that the point now sits on the vertical crease just made.

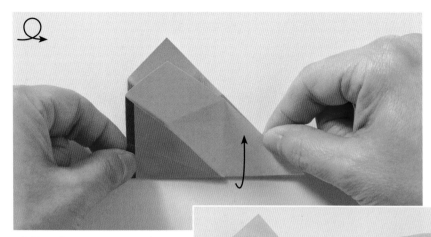

4 Turn the paper over and fold it in half from bottom to top, then turn the right-hand point back across the vertical crease and tuck it behind the diagonal flap.

5 Fold down the upper sheet from the top at an angle, so that the corner of the flap now sits on the bottom right-hand corner.

6 Turn the paper over and fold the top point over at an angle to the bottom left corner.

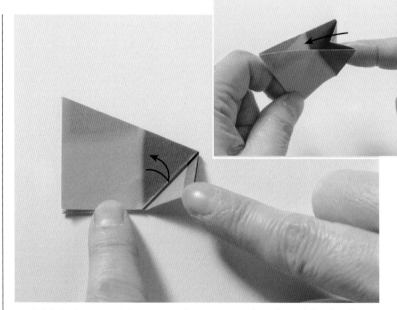

7 Fold the bottom right corner of paper over the edge of the flap just made to form a crease, then lift up the paper and open it out slightly to let you push the corner back inside the model.

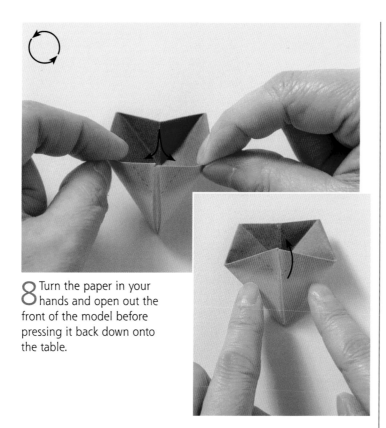

8 Turn the paper in your hands and open out the front of the model before pressing it back down onto the table.

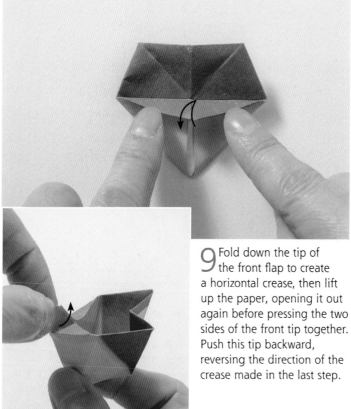

9 Fold down the tip of the front flap to create a horizontal crease, then lift up the paper, opening it out again before pressing the two sides of the front tip together. Push this tip backward, reversing the direction of the crease made in the last step.

10 Make up the other seven pieces of paper in the same way then use the paper glue to stick them together in a circle to form the sea anemone.

13 ZARUGAI | SCALLOP

The scallop has no tentacles, arms, or legs, but lives 150 feet (45 meters) under the suface on the seabed. They are characterized by radial patterns on the surface of their shell. The trick to complete this model is to fold the diagonal folds as tightly as possible to create a three-dimensional effect.

You will need:
1 sheet of 6in (15cm) origami paper

Difficulty rating: ● ● ○

IN THE ROCK POOL

1 With the design side down, fold the paper in half from corner to corner across the design to make a crease and open out. Fold between the other corners then lift the left-hand corner, open out the flap, and press forward into a diamond. Turn the paper over and repeat.

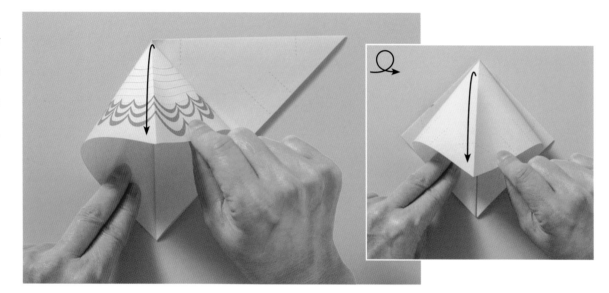

2 Fold in the lower diagonal edges of the top layer of paper so that they meet in the middle, then turn the top point down over the edges of these flaps to make a horizontal crease.

3 Open up the flaps and push the corner of paper up and over the top to form a long diamond shape, reversing the direction of the creases where necessary.

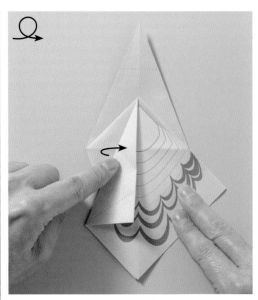

4 Turn the paper over and fold in the upper edges of the diamond shape so that the edges meet along the central crease.

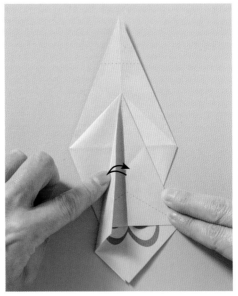

5 Fold the same sides over again so that they also meet along the central crease.

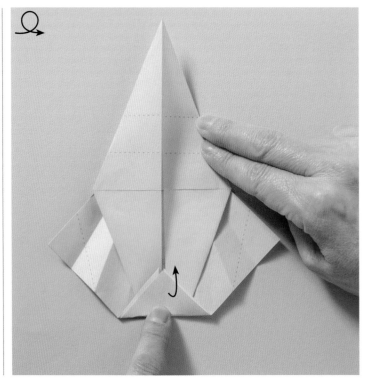

6 Open out the last two folds made and turn the paper over, then fold up the bottom point using the marks printed on the paper as a guide.

7 Fold the side points in at an angle using the marks on the paper as a guide.

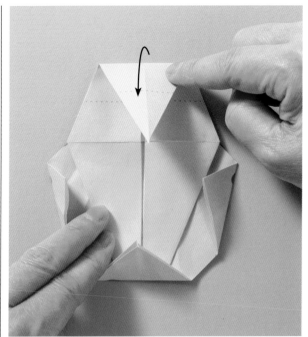

8 Turn over the top point using the upper set of marks as a guide.

9 Turn the same flap over again using the lower set of marks printed on the paper, then fold the protruding point of paper over the edge just made.

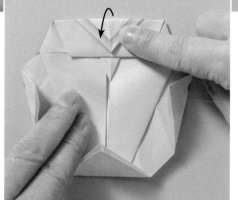

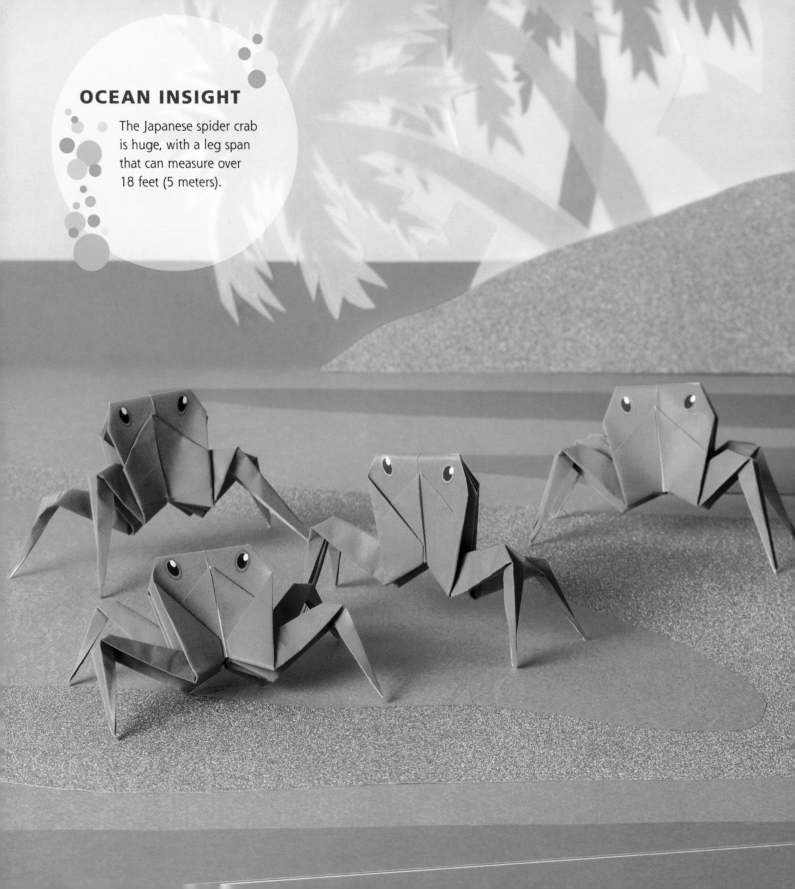

OCEAN INSIGHT

The Japanese spider crab is huge, with a leg span that can measure over 18 feet (5 meters).

14 KANI | CRAB

Crabs are fascinating creatures that can be seen in every size and shape, though they all scuttle sideways at great speed across the beach and through the water. This origami model demonstrates its agility, with its long, thin legs that are surprisingly strong. To make an accurate origami crab, try folding the sides of the body into the center line softly to bring a greater realism to the model.

You will need:
1 sheet of 6in (15cm) origami paper

Difficulty rating: ● ● ●

1 With the design side down, fold the paper in half from corner to corner across the design to make a crease and open out. Fold between the other corners then lift the right-hand corner, open out the flap, and press forward into a diamond. Turn the paper over and repeat.

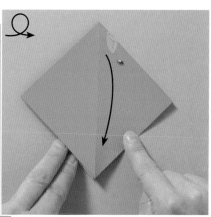

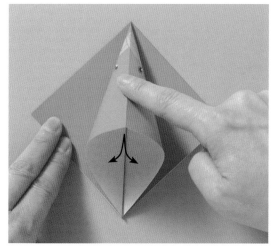

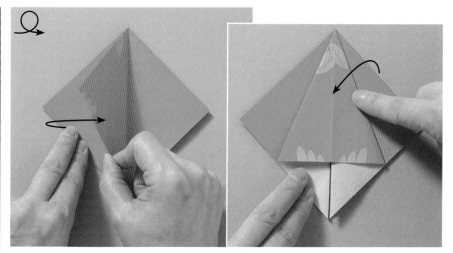

2 Lift up the right-hand flap and open out the pocket, pressing the paper flat.

3 Turn the paper over and lift the right-hand flap, again opening it out and pressing it flat into a triangle shape.

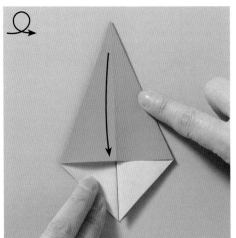

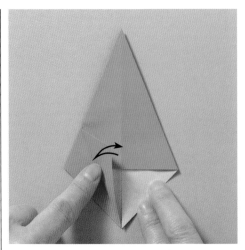

4 Close up the triangle just made by turning the right-hand side over to the left, then lift the left-hand point and also open this up before pressing it down into a triangle.

5 Turn the paper over and close up the triangle showing the design of the face by turning the right-hand side over to the left. Then pick up the last remaining flap on the right, open this up, and press it flat in the same way.

6 Fold over the lower diagonal edges on both sides so that they meet along the central crease.

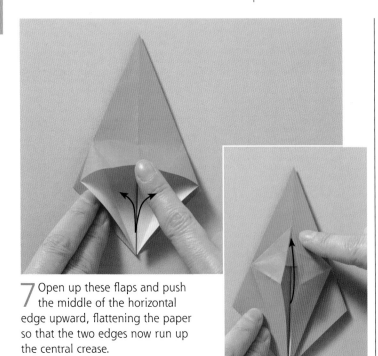

7 Open up these flaps and push the middle of the horizontal edge upward, flattening the paper so that the two edges now run up the central crease.

8 Turn the paper over and repeat steps 6 and 7, then turn over the left-hand flap to reveal the third triangle to be transformed into a diamond shape.

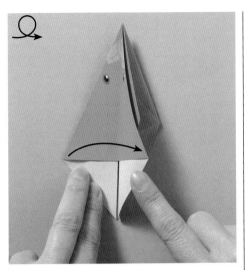

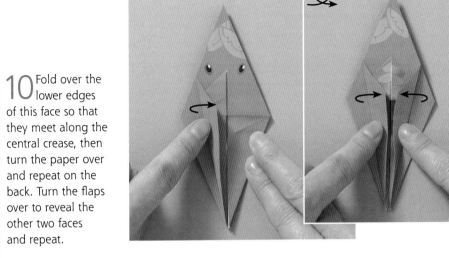

10 Fold over the lower edges of this face so that they meet along the central crease, then turn the paper over and repeat on the back. Turn the flaps over to reveal the other two faces and repeat.

9 Turn the paper over again and fold over the last flap to reveal the design of the crab's face. Repeat steps 6 and 7.

12 Carefully open out each leg and fold the tip down inside at an angle, again reversing the direction of the central crease. Repeat on the other three legs, then turn the paper over and turn back the top point to make the top of the head flat.

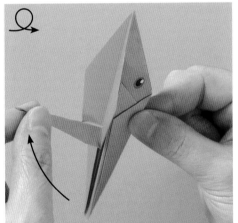

11 With the eyes front again lift up the paper and open up the first flap on the left. Lift the point to the horizontal, then press the flap shut again forming new folds and reversing the direction of the crease along the length of the leg. Repeat on the other three flaps.

13 UMI ZARIGANI | LOBSTER

The lobster is a type of crayfish that lives in the sea and is often seen as a powerful hunter due to its hammer-like scissor pincers. This origami model also emphasizes those scissors. As these can be tricky to fold, ask an adult for some help when you make the model for the first time.

You will need:
1 sheet of 6in (15cm) origami paper

Difficulty rating: ● ● ●

1 With the design side down, fold the paper in half from corner to corner through the design, then lift the left-hand corner to the vertical, open out the flap, and press forward into a diamond. Turn the paper over and repeat.

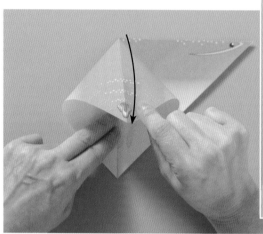

2 Turn the lower edges of the uppermost flap over to meet along the central crease, then turn the top point over the edges of these flaps to form a crease before opening up the flaps and lifting the bottom point of paper, turning it back over to the top to form a diamond shape.

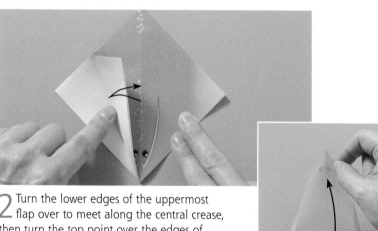
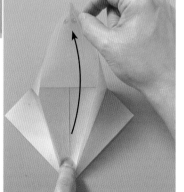

3 Turn the paper over and repeat.

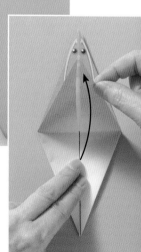

IN THE ROCK POOL

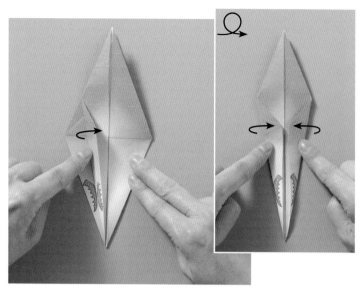

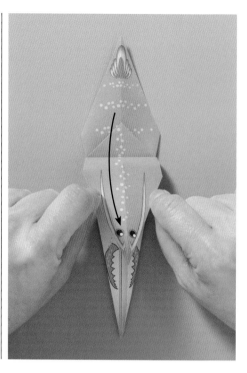

4 Fold in the lower edges of the uppermost flaps so that they meet along the central crease, then turn the paper over and repeat on the other side.

5 Fold down the top point to reveal the design for the face, making a horizontal crease as far down as possible.

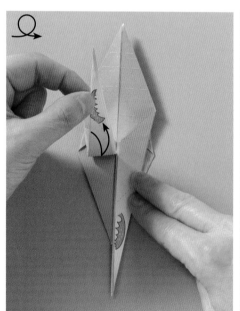

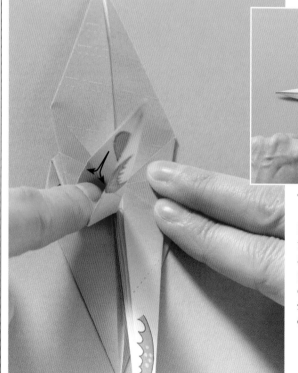

6 Turn the paper over and lift the left-hand point to the vertical.

7 Gently open up the flap by inserting a finger into the pocket before pushing downward, so forming two small diagonal creases at the base of the flap. Push the point out to the side and back down to the table, using the two small creases as fold lines. Repeat on the right-hand side.

8 Fold the top point down, using the marks printed on the design as a guide, before turning the tip back to create a concertina fold.

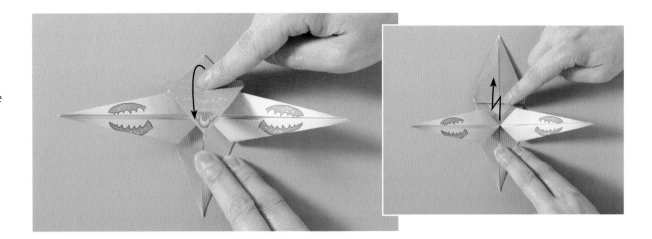

9 Make three more concertina folds up the same flap using the marks printed on the design to show their positions.

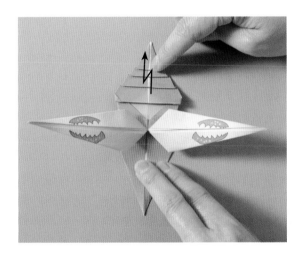

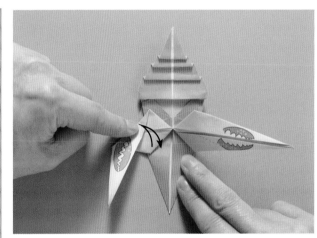

10 Next, fold the arms forward at an angle.

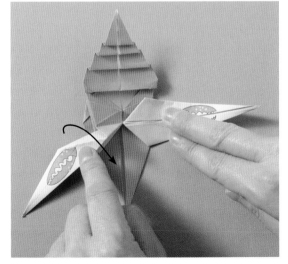

11 Fold forward the point at the inner end of the long flap's upper edge, closing the flap to form the angled shape of the claw.

PART THREE

AROUND THE REEF

16 KUMANOMI | CLOWN FISH

You will need:
1 sheet of 6in (15cm) origami paper

Difficulty rating: ● ○ ○

The clown fish lives among the coral reefs of the tropical Indian and Pacific Oceans. Its characteristic stripy body with orange, white, and black stripes makes it instantly recognizable as well as easy to spot as it zips though the water. The clown fish model is simple so make lots of them with your friends!

1 With the design face down, fold the paper in half from side to side both ways, opening out each time. Fold in the left-hand edge to the vertical crease to make another crease, then fold the edge in to this last crease.

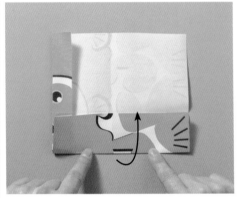

2 Fold the top and bottom edges in to meet along the central crease.

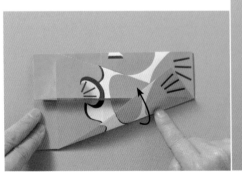

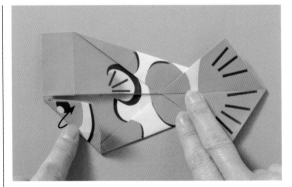

3 Turn over the right-hand corners at an angle, using the marks printed on the design as a guide, then turn back the corners so that the folded edges meet along the central crease.

4 Turn over the two left-hand corners at an angle to finish.

OCEAN INSIGHT

Rather unusually, male sea horses carry eggs and some can give birth to over 1,000 baby sea horses at a time.

17 TATSUNOOTOSHIGO | SEA HORSE

You will need:
1 sheet of 6in (15cm) origami paper

Difficulty rating: ● ● ●

The sea horse is a saltwater fish that lives in shallow waters around coasts and reefs. Due to its unique body shape, in Japan its name actually translates as "baby of a dragon." A good tip to remember when making this model is to bend the lower body to achieve a realistic look.

1 With the design face down, fold the paper in half from corner to corner through the design to make a crease and open out. Fold in the two lower edges so that they meet along the central crease, then fold in the two shorter upper edges in the same way.

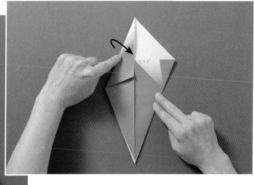

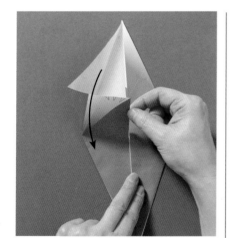

2 Open the last flap and lift the corner of paper up to the vertical.

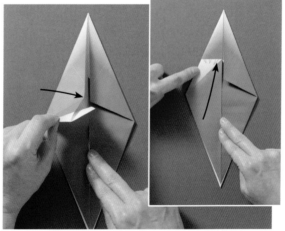

3 Push the edge of paper back down into the center of the paper, then fold the corner of paper back down in place, reversing the direction of the creases.

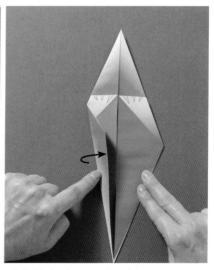

4 Fold the lower edges in to the center.

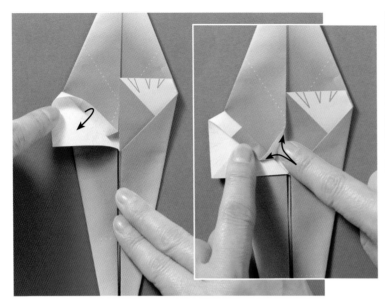

5 Fold the corner of paper underneath the left-hand flap back over the flap's diagonal edge and press down, turning the extra narrow strip of paper with it. Press down the inner turn of paper, using the marks printed on the paper as a guide, to create an irregular-shaped triangle. Repeat on the other side.

6 Fold up the bottom point across the flaps' horizontal edges to make a crease, then turn the flap back in a concertina fold.

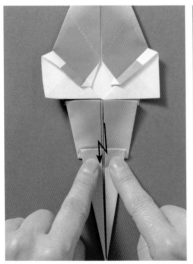

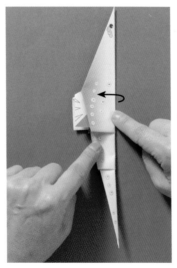

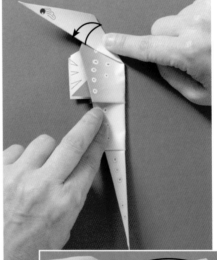

7 Make a second concertina fold nearer the bottom tip, using the marks printed on the paper as a guide.

8 Fold the model in half along its length.

9 Fold over the top point to make a diagonal crease, using the marks on the paper as a guide, then open up the body and fold the point inside along this crease, reversing the direction of the fold as necessary.

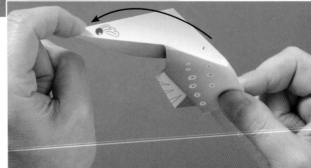

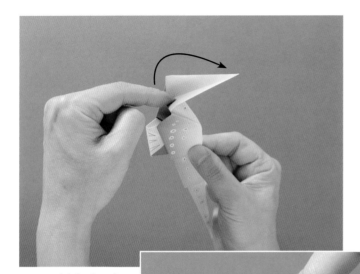

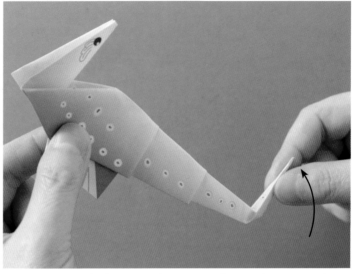

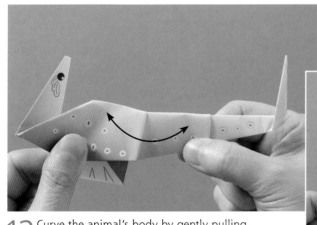

10 Fold the head back over on itself so that it points in the opposite direction, then fold back the tip of the nose and press it inside the head.

11 Turn over the bottom point at an angle to make a crease then refold the tip around the body, reversing the direction of the creases as necessary.

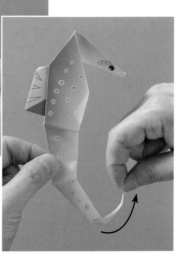

12 Curve the animal's body by gently pulling apart the concertina folds then finish by giving the tail an extra crease.

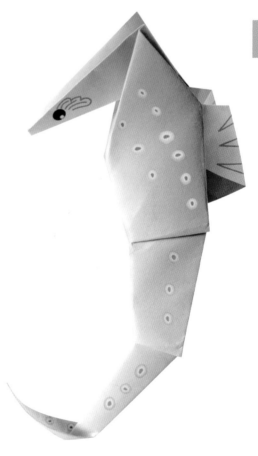

TATSUNOOTOSHIGO | SEA HORSE

18 KIROHAGI | YELLOW TANG

You will need:
1 sheet of 6in (15cm) origami paper

Difficulty rating: ● ○ ○

As its name suggests, the yellow tang is a beautiful yellow, vivid fish. It is well known because it is often seen in aquariums but it also gives beautiful displays in its natural habitat, whizzing among the coral. Making this origami model is very simple, so why not make a whole group with which you can start to populate your very own origami aquarium.

1 Fold the paper in half from top to bottom then fold the left-hand side over again. Lift this flap to the vertical, open it out and press flat into a triangle.

2 Turn the paper over and repeat, then fold over the left-hand flap at an angle, using the marks printed on the paper as a guide.

3 Repeat on the right-hand flap, then turn the remaining flap on the left over so that the point sits at the bottom of the previous flap made and leaves a vertical edge.

4 Fold back the tip to make a large concertina fold then repeat this and the previous step on the remaining flap.

OCEAN INSIGHT

Yellow tangs change color over the course of a day, becoming less bright at night to make them less visible to predators.

19 NANYOHAGI | BLUE TANG

You will need:
1 sheet of 6in (15cm) origami paper

Difficulty rating: ● ○ ○

Like the yellow tang and clown fish, the blue tang lives in tropical reefs, eating algae growing on the coral to survive. However, unlike clown fish, the blue tang has beautiful iridescent blue, black, and yellow markings. This model is simple to make, so have a go!

1 With the design face down, fold the paper in half through the design to make a crease and open out. Turn over the left-hand point to make a vertical fold, using the marks printed on the paper as a guide.

2 Turn the bottom and top points into the center at an angle, again using the marks printed on the paper as a guide.

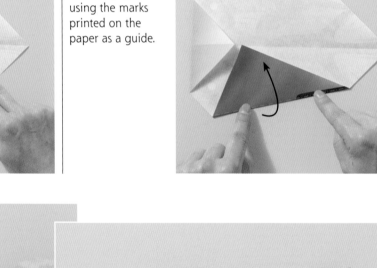

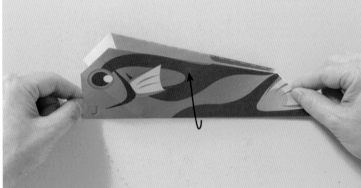

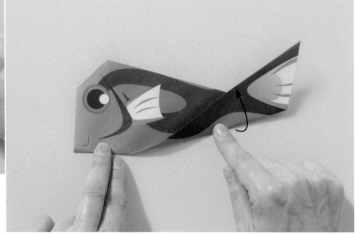

3 Fold the model in half along its length, then finish by turning over the tail at an angle along the line marked on the paper.

20 **YAKO** | ANGELFISH

Another relative of the clown fish and blue tang is the angelfish and, like them, it also lives in small shoals among the coral of the reef. The similarities don't stop there: angelfish are very popular aquarium fish because of their vivid colors and long, floating fins, which stream through the water as they swim.

You will need:
1 sheet of 6in (15cm) origami paper

Difficulty rating: ● ● ○

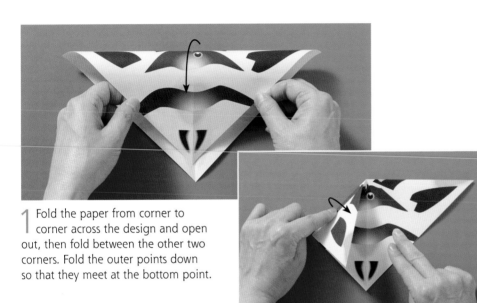

1 Fold the paper from corner to corner across the design and open out, then fold between the other two corners. Fold the outer points down so that they meet at the bottom point.

2 Fold these same flaps in half so that the vertical edge runs along the outer crease on both sides.

3 Lift and open these flaps and refold them, pressing them flat into a diamond shape.

4 Turn over the outer edges of the flaps so that they meet along the center of the diamond.

5 Open out these flaps and push the tip up and back, ensuring that the edges of paper meet evenly down the middle of the diamond.

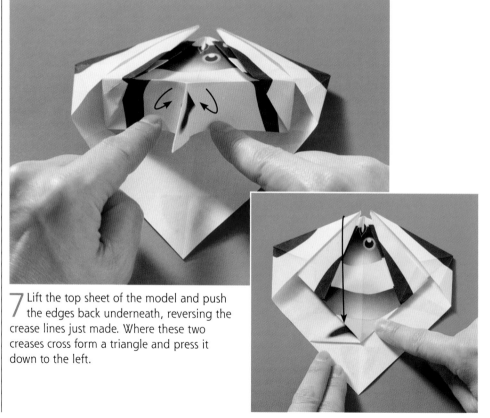

6 Fold over the edges of the uppermost sheet on both sides, including the inside of each diamond shape, to make new crease lines parallel to the outer edge.

7 Lift the top sheet of the model and push the edges back underneath, reversing the crease lines just made. Where these two creases cross form a triangle and press it down to the left.

8 Turn back the tips of the two diamonds to reveal the design.

There are over 80 different species of marine angelfish and they are some of the most colorful fish in the ocean.

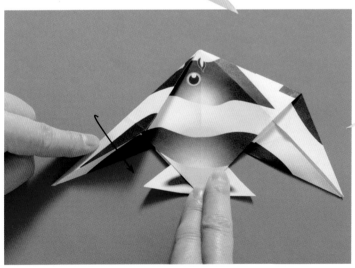

9 Turn the paper over and make two creases to match those made in step 6, then carefully fold the edges back inside the model, again pointing the triangle that is formed at their intersection to the left.

10 Finish by folding the outer diamonds in half along their central crease.

21 MIDORIFUGU | PUFFERFISH

You will need:
1 sheet of 6in (15cm) origami paper

Difficulty rating: ● ● ○

Usually pufferfish are small, slim-looking and unremarkable fish but their unique point of interest is that they can "puff" up their body into a large, round ball to scare away a potential predator. Like the traditional balloon origami, this model is complete once it is inflated.

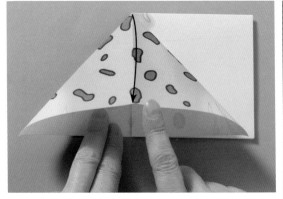

1 Fold the paper in half from top to bottom, then fold the left-hand side over again. Lift this flap to the vertical, open it out, and press flat into a triangle.

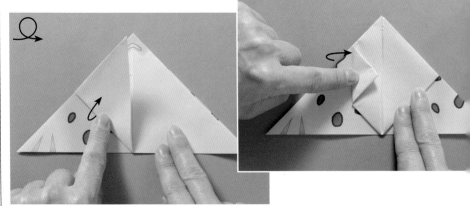

2 Turn the paper over and repeat, then fold the top layer of the outer points up to the top to create a diamond shape. Fold in the outer points so that they meet on the central crease, forming triangles.

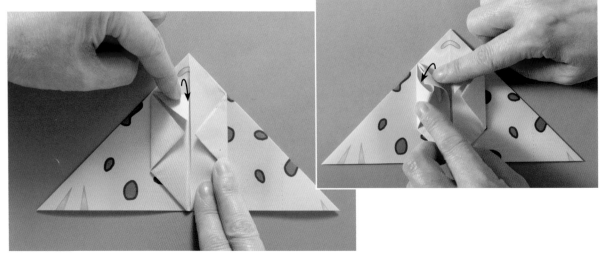

3 Fold down both sides of the diamond's top point then, using the diagonal edge of this new flap as a fold line, tuck the flap into the pocket along the top edge of the original triangle.

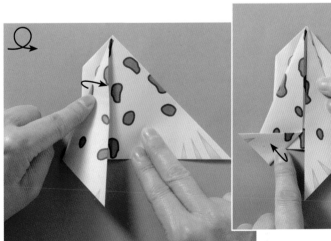

4 Turn the paper over and fold the diagonal edges in so that they meet along the central crease. Fold the bottom points of these flaps up and out at right angles to form the fish's tail.

5 Pick up the paper and prise the sides apart, then gently blow into the model to form its shape.

22 MANBOH | SUNFISH

You will need:
1 sheet of 6in (15cm) origami paper

Difficulty rating: ● ○ ○

Is that a UFO flying under the sea? No, it is only a sunfish—a unique creature with a wide flat, body which, unlike the other fish on the reef, can be many times bigger than a man. They use their unique physique to drift effortlessly through the water, so let's try and recreate this extraordinary fish in an origami model.

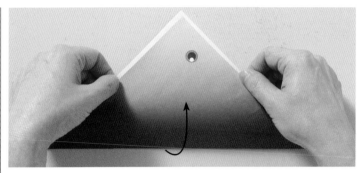

1 With the design face down, fold the paper in half from corner to corner through the design.

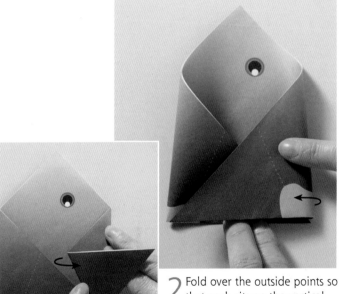

2 Fold over the outside points so that each sits on the vertical edge made by the other flap. Next, turn back the points at the angle shown by the marks printed on the design.

3 Fold back the top point to make the fish's snout.

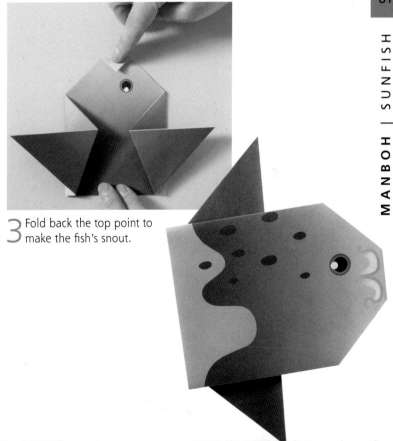

23 TAKO | OCTOPUS

You will need:
1 sheet of 6in (15cm) origami paper
Scissors

Difficulty rating: ● ● ●

The octopus has eight, long sinuous tentacles that are covered in suckers. It uses them both to move stealthily through the water and also to catch hold of anything it wants under the sea. The process of making an octopus origami is very similar to a traditional origami crane, but remember to curl the tentacles when you have finished to give it some life of its own.

1 With the design face down, fold the paper in half from corner to corner across the design to make a crease and open out. Fold between the other corners, then lift the left-hand corner, open out the flap, and press forward into a diamond. Turn the paper over and repeat.

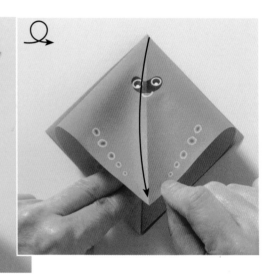

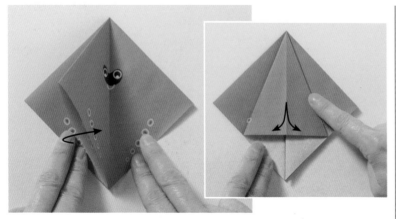

2 Lift the left-hand flap to the vertical, open the pocket, and press down to form a triangle.

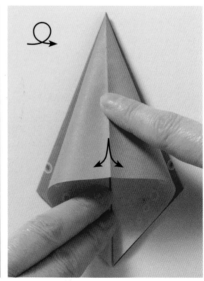

3 Turn the paper over and repeat. Repeat on the other two faces, turning the paper over each time.

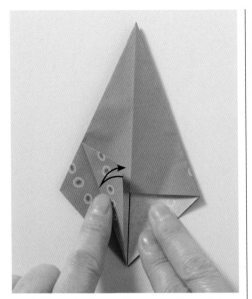

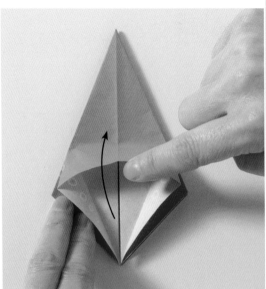

4 Fold up the lower diagonal edges of the uppermost flaps on both sides so that they meet along the central crease.

5 Open up the flaps and push the middle of the horizontal edge up and away so that the edges of paper now meet each other up the central crease. Repeat three times around the model.

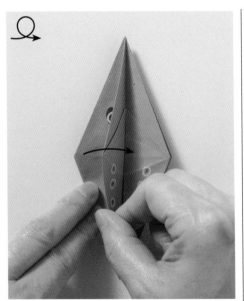

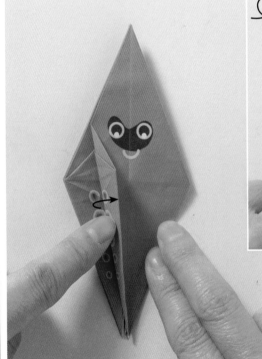

6 Turn the left-hand flap to the right to reveal the design for the face.

7 Fold in the lower edges so that they meet along the central crease. Repeat on the other three sides, turning the model over as needed.

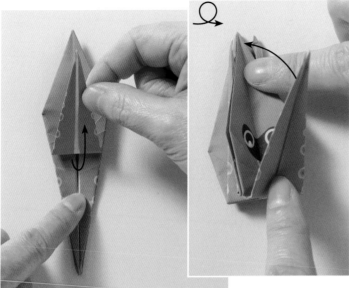

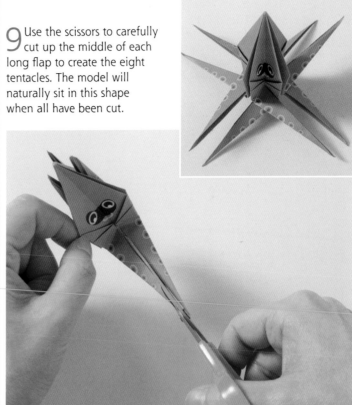

9 Use the scissors to carefully cut up the middle of each long flap to create the eight tentacles. The model will naturally sit in this shape when all have been cut.

8 Fold up each point, making a horizontal crease as high up the model as possible, turning the paper over as necessary.

10 Carefully pull open each face, ensuring that you don't open up the tentacles as you work. Finish by curling the tentacles around a pencil to give them some shape.

OCEAN INSIGHT

Sea angels get their name from the set of "wings" used to help them swim.

24 HADAKA KAMEGAI | SEA ANGEL

You will need:
1 sheet of 6in (15cm) origami paper

Difficulty rating: ● ● ●

Sea angels are mysterious and confusing creatures: they are very similar to sea slugs but are almost completely transparent and they do not move around the ocean floor but float in the water, drifting with the current on a pair of wings. Though this project can be tricky, be brave and have a go!

1 With the design face down, fold the paper in half from corner to corner across the design to make a crease and open out. Fold between the other corners, then lift the left-hand corner, open out the flap, and press forward into a diamond. Turn the paper over and repeat.

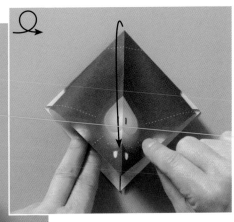

2 Fold in the lower edges of the uppermost flap so that they meet along the central crease, then fold down the top point over the edges of these flaps to make a crease.

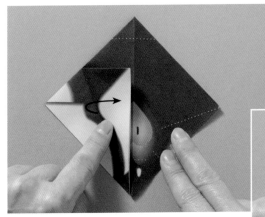

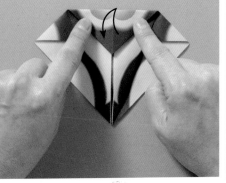

3 Open out the flaps and lift the corner of paper over the top to form a long diamond shape.

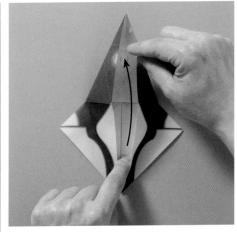

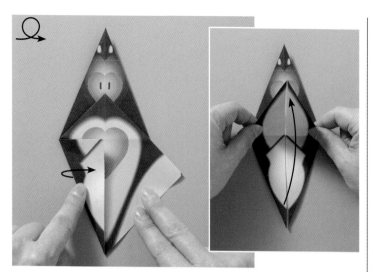

4 Turn the paper over and repeat, folding in the lower edges and making a horizontal crease before opening the flaps out and turning the point of paper over the top to create a diamond.

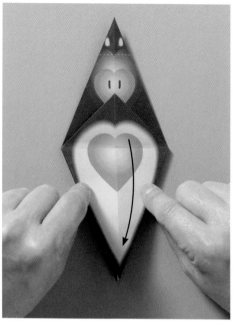

5 Take the upper sheet from the top point and fold it back down to the bottom of the model.

6 Turn the paper over and lift it off the table, holding the right-hand lower edge in your right hand and the top layer of the lower left-hand flap in your left.

7 Carefully lift up the left-hand flap so that the point now points out horizontally to the left. Press the flap down so that the new creases you have just made are folded up behind the flap. Repeat on the right-hand side.

8 Refold the creases behind the upper part of the flap, using the marks printed on the paper as a guide.

9 Fold down the top point, using the lower line marked on the paper as a guide, then turn it back up using the higher line to form the sea angel's head.

10 Turn the model over and tuck the top point of the body behind itself.

11 Finish by turning the point at the top of the wing out from the body, opening up the small pocket, and push down flat so that the bottom corners cover the central diamond.

PART FOUR

IN THE DEEP

OCEAN INSIGHT

Dolphins like to play. They have been known to surf waves and have even been filmed playing makeshift ball games in the sea.

25 IRUKA | DOLPHIN

Dolphins are incredibly intelligent and sociable. They can often be seen swimming alongside boats in groups known as pods and can be taught to perform tricks. This model is based on techniques that are often used when folding origami fish. Forming the fin might be tricky, but don't be scared to give it a go!

You will need:
1 sheet of 6in (15cm) origami paper

Difficulty rating: ● ● ○

1 With the design face down, fold the paper in half from corner to corner through the design to make a crease and open out. Fold in the left-hand edges so that they meet along the central crease, then turn the paper over and fold the narrow point over to the other side.

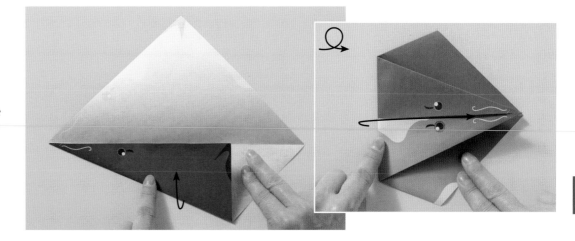

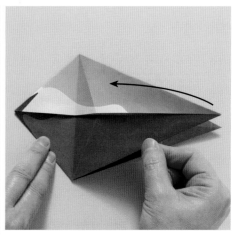

2 Turn the paper back over and lift the lower flap, then take it out to the left of the model, refolding to form a triangle-shaped flap.

3 Lift the upper layer from the right-hand side and turn it over to the left.

4 Turn back the right-hand point and make a crease, using the marks printed on the paper as a guide, then turn the point back to form a concertina fold.

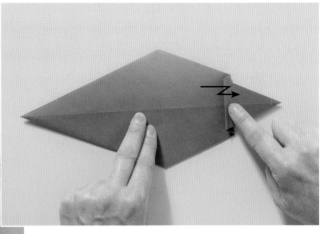

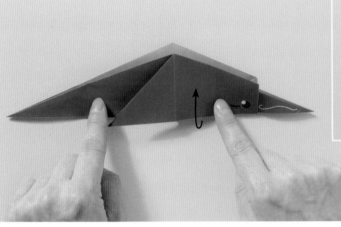

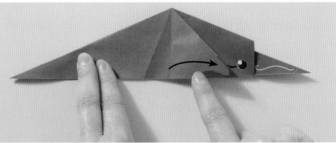

5 Fold the model in half along its length, then turn forward the triangular flap on the side.

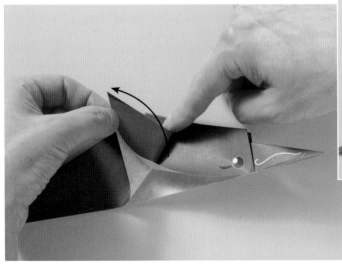

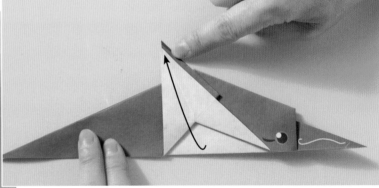

6 Place a finger near the top of the flap's diagonal edge, then turn it up and over the top of the paper at an angle, pressing down to form new creases.

7 Turn the paper over and fold the triangular flap in half so that the diagonal edge runs vertically up the crease behind then fold the whole flap forward.

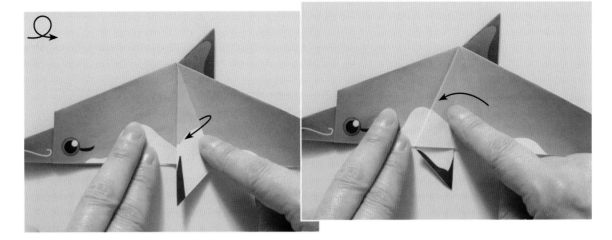

8 Turn up the right-hand point at an angle to make a crease then refold it inside, reversing the direction of the creases as necessary, to form the tail.

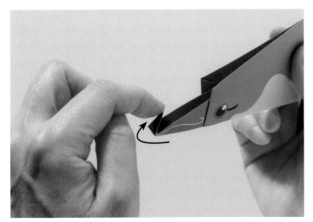

9 Turn back the left-hand end and fold it inside to form the nose.

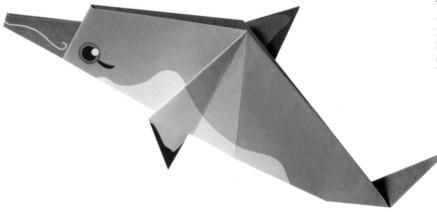

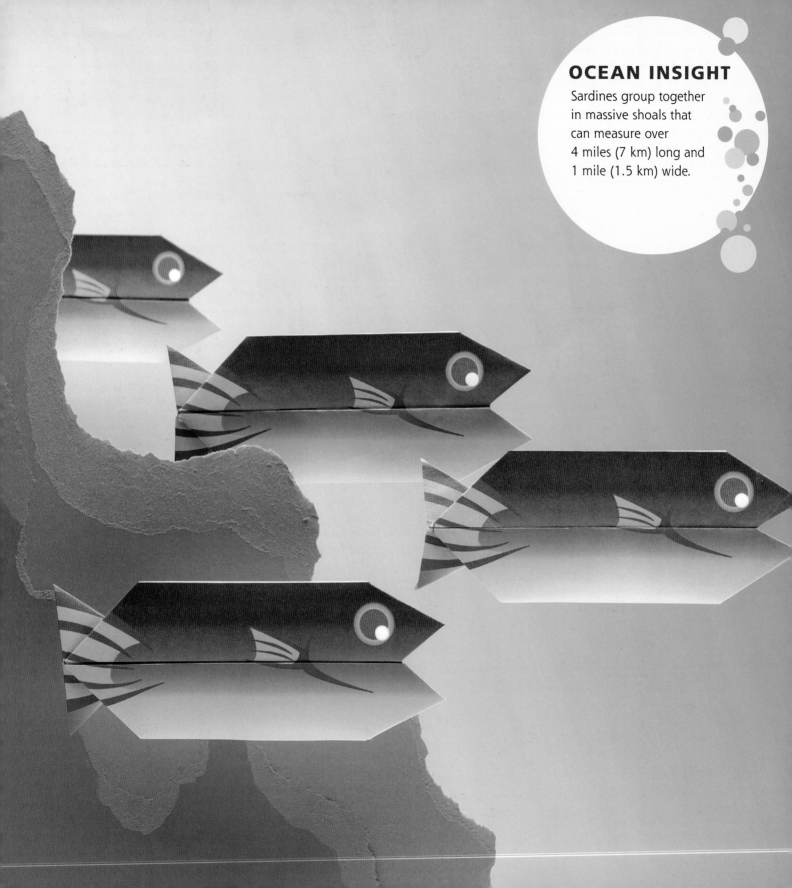

26 IWASHI | SARDINE

Sardines are small fish that live in huge shoals to protect themselves from bigger fish, swimming near the surface of the sea along coasts around the world. Although the tail and the beak of this model are a little difficult to make, take care to look at the pictures in the steps and fold carefully.

You will need:
1 sheet of 6in (15cm) origami paper

Difficulty rating: ● ● ●

1 Fold over the left-hand side of the paper, using the marks printed on the design as a guide, then turn the flap back on itself so that the edges align.

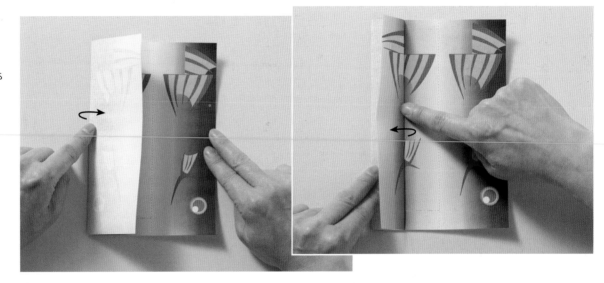

2 Repeat on the other side, ensuring that the folded edges run down the center of the paper.

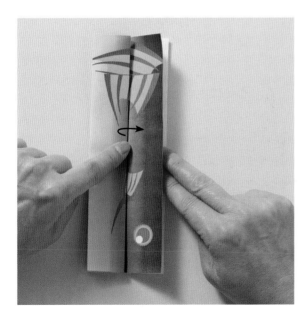

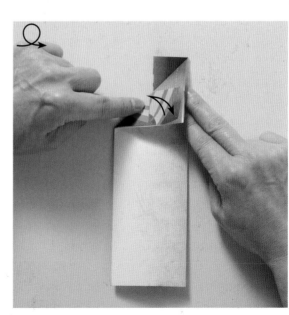

3 Turn the paper over and fold over the top corners to make diagonal creases.

4 Use the creases just made to fold in the sides of the paper, pressing just above the points where the diagonal creases meet the edges, leaving several layers of paper standing vertical. Carefully open up the central pocket of these sheets and press flat.

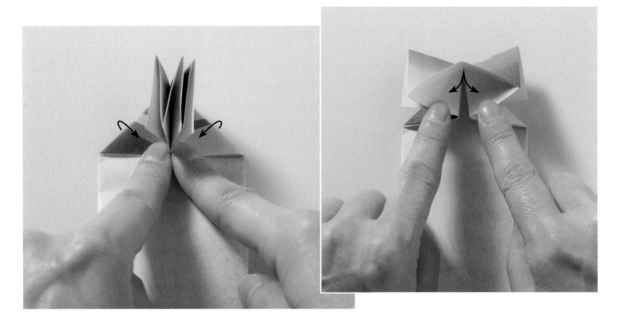

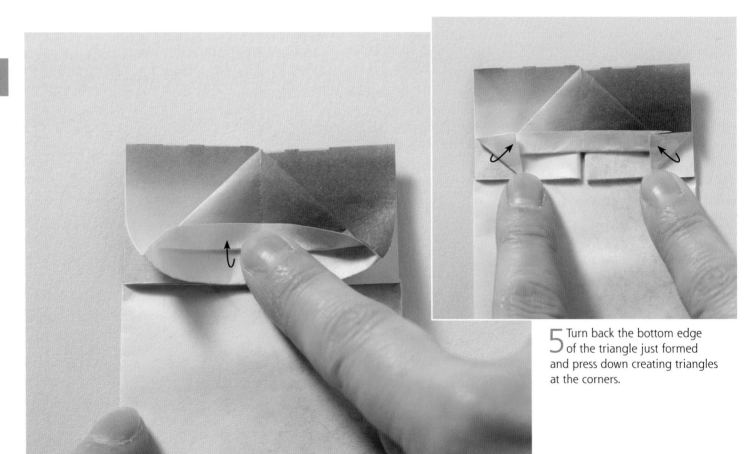

5 Turn back the bottom edge of the triangle just formed and press down creating triangles at the corners.

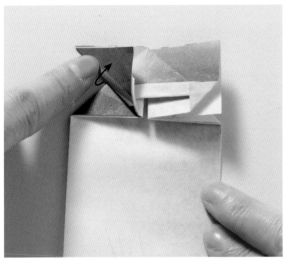

6 Turn over the bottom corners of the flaps, making new diagonal fold lines.

7 At the other end carefully lift the uppermost edge of the paper and fold back, again creating new creases and triangular folds on either side.

8 Turn back the inner corners of the new flaps at an angle, then turn over the bottom corners so that the horizontal edges now run along the angled creases just made.

27 KUJIRA | WHALE

Whales, the largest mammals in the world, live in almost every part of the ocean. Most are fish and meat eaters and some have bristle-like teeth to catch and filter thousands of plankton or krill with every mouthful. This model is simple to make and, by opening the model slightly, it successfully gives an impression of its huge size.

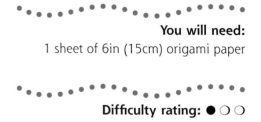

You will need:
1 sheet of 6in (15cm) origami paper

Difficulty rating: ● ○ ○

IN THE DEEP

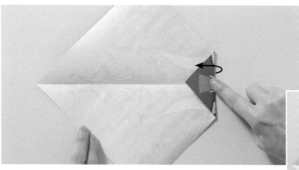

1 Fold the paper in half from corner to corner through the design to make a crease. Open out, then fold in the right-hand point and then the top and bottom points.

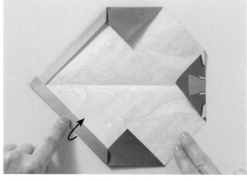

2 Fold over the left-hand edges, using the marks printed on the paper as a guide.

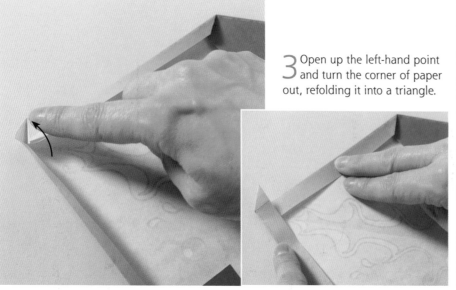

3 Open up the left-hand point and turn the corner of paper out, refolding it into a triangle.

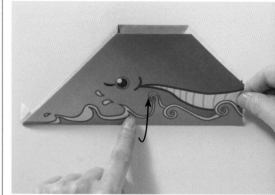

4 Finish by folding the paper in half horizontally.

OCEAN INSIGHT

The biggest animal in the world is the blue whale, which is almost 100 feet (30 meters) long.

28 IKA | SQUID

Like the octopus, the squid's body is boneless but it is made of muscle and the animal can travel through the water at great speed. Its main source of food is small fish and crustaceans, which it captures in its long tentacles. If you make the squid using plain origami paper you can draw your own face and markings on the model when you have finished.

You will need:

1 sheet of 6in (15cm) origami paper

Difficulty rating: ● ● ○

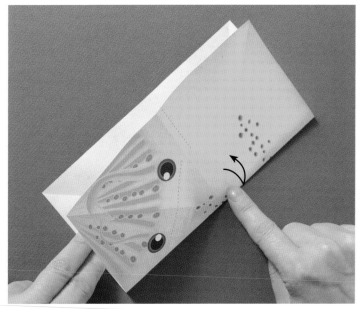

1 With the design face down, fold the paper in half from corner to corner both ways to make creases, opening out each time, then repeat from side to side both ways, opening out again.

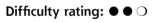

2 Fold over the top left edge so that it runs along the central crease, then repeat on the right-hand side.

3 Open up the flaps just made and release the corner of paper from inside. Fold the flaps back in place, leaving the corner of paper standing vertical.

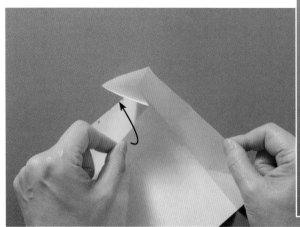

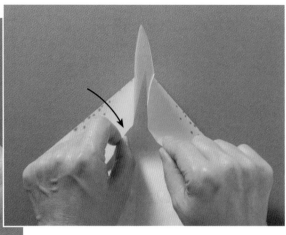

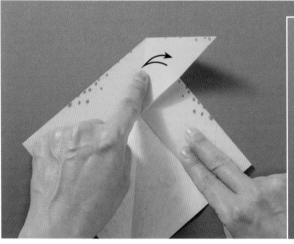

4 Fold the flap over to the right to form a crease, then open out the flap and press it down flat, forming a diamond shape.

5 Fold in the lower edges so that the meet along the central crease.

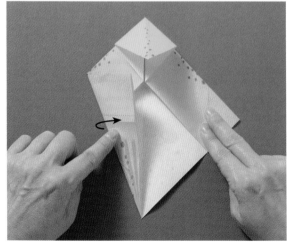

6 Fold the diamond-shaped flap back to the right, reforming the triangle shape.

7 Fold over the upper edges so that they meet along the central crease, turning the triangular flaps to the left to give access to the right-hand side before returning it to the diamond form.

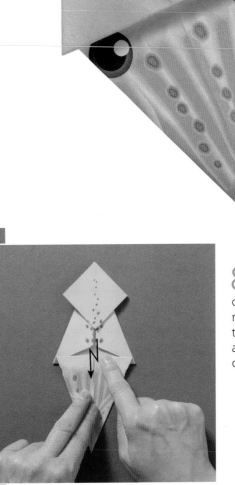

8 Fold up the bottom point making a crease between the model's outer points, then fold the tip back again, creating a concertina fold.

29 SAME | SHARK

If you see a fin breaking the surface of the water you know the most feared predator in the sea, the shark, is close by. However, not all are dangerous and the very largest only eat plankton. This model is as simple as can be with both sides ending up symmetrical to each other.

You will need:
1 sheet of 6in (15cm) origami paper

Difficulty rating: ● ○ ○

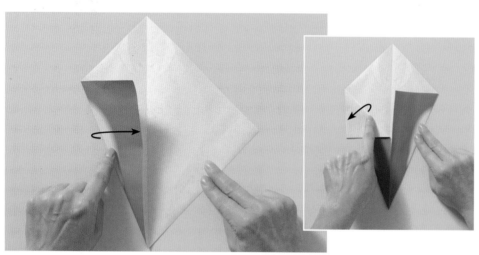

1 Fold the paper in half from corner to corner through the design to make a crease and open out. Fold over the lower edges so that they meet along the central crease. Next turn back the corners of the new flaps into triangles.

2 Fold in the top corners of the new flaps, using the marks printed on the paper as a guide.

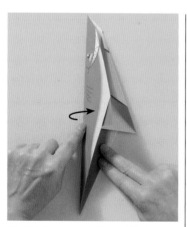

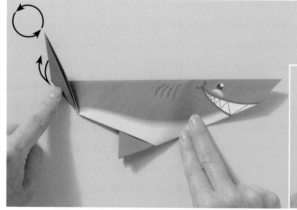

3 Fold the model in half along the central crease.

4 Spin the paper through 90 degrees, then turn up the left-hand point at an angle to make a crease. Lift up the paper and carefully fold the point around the rest of the model, reversing the direction of the creases as necessary.

OCEAN INSIGHT

A shark can lose up to 30,000 teeth in a lifetime. This is because shark teeth are attached to the gums rather than the jaws. When a tooth falls out, the ones behind move forward and new one is grown to replace it.

30 IKAKU | NARWHAL

The narwhal lives in the Arctic waters and is often referred to as the "unicorn of the sea" with its long pointed tusk and pale skin. To successfully make this narwhal the best tip is to make a firm crease along the dotted line so that the horn is nice and strong.

You will need:
1 sheet of 6in (15cm) origami paper
Scissors

Difficulty rating: ● ○ ○

1 Fold the paper in half from corner to corner through the design to make a crease and open out. Fold over the lower edges so that they meet along the central crease.

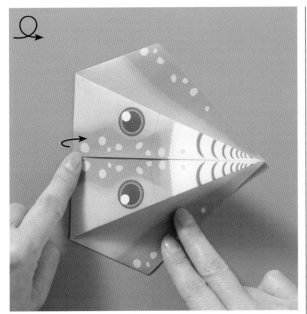

2 Turn the paper over and fold the narrow point over from the left to the right.

3 Turn the paper over again, spin it through 180 degrees, then lift the corner of the upper flap, turning it out to the right and reforming the flap into a triangle. Repeat on the bottom flap then turn the flap on the left over to the right.

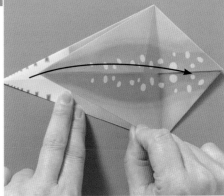

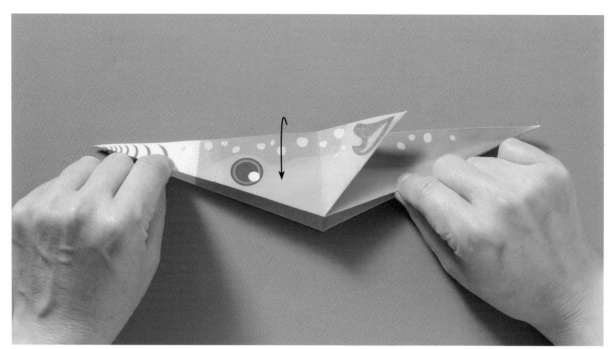

4 Fold the model in half along its central crease.

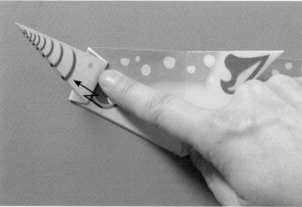

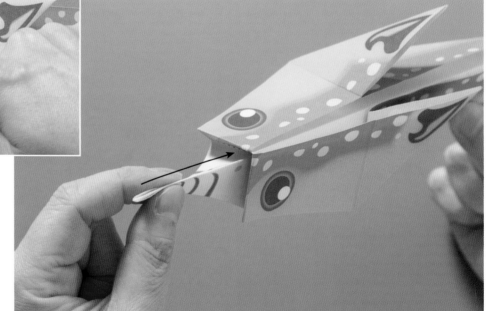

5 Fold over the left-hand point, using the marks printed on the paper as a guide, then turn it back again to form a concertina fold. Carefully open up the model and refold the tip inside, reversing the direction of the creases as necessary.

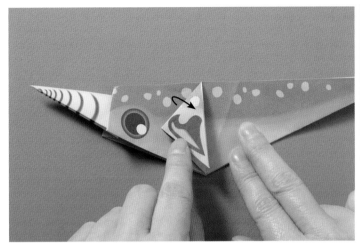

6 Fold the triangular flap in the center to the left, then halve it by running the horizontal edge down the vertical crease. Turn over and repeat on the other side.

7 Open up the model and use the scissors to carefully cut along the central crease from the right-hand point.

OCEAN INSIGHT

The narwhal's distinctive tusk (which is actually a tooth) can grow to a length of around 10 feet (3 meters).

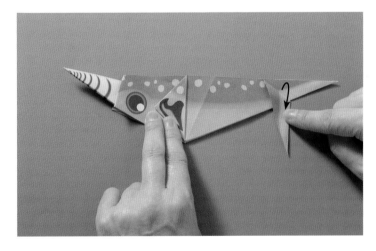

8 Turn over the top layer of the right-hand point to form the tail.

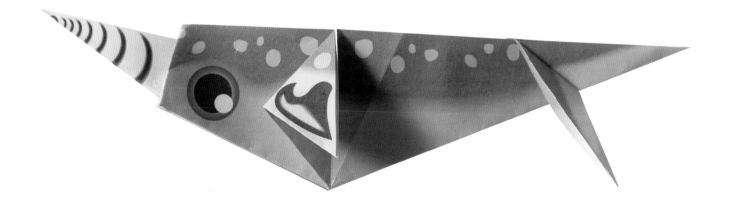

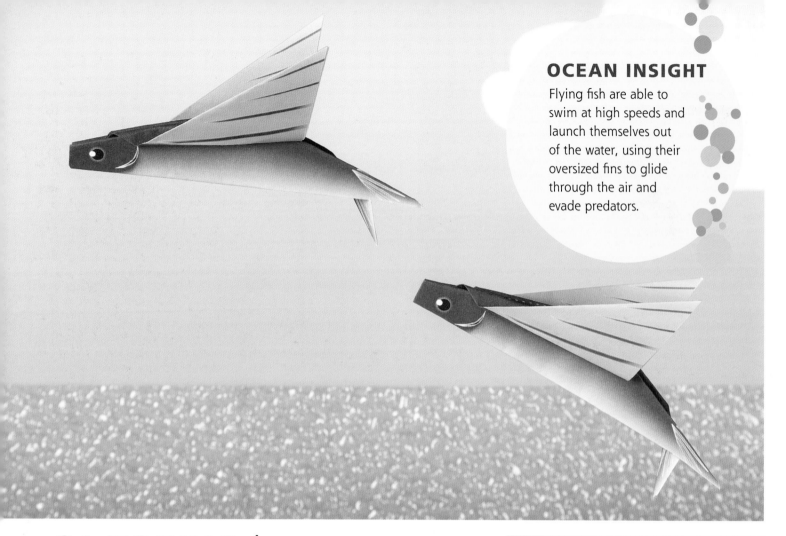

OCEAN INSIGHT

Flying fish are able to swim at high speeds and launch themselves out of the water, using their oversized fins to glide through the air and evade predators.

31 TOBIUO | FLYING FISH

Can a fish fly? Yes, a flying fish can! It launches itself out of the water and spreads its long, thin fins like wings to glide across the surface. Remember to fold accurately along the dotted lines with a little force.

You will need:

1 sheet of 6in (15cm) origami paper
Scissors

Difficulty rating: ● ○ ○

1 With the design face down, fold the paper in half through the design to make a crease and open out. Repeat in the other direction, then turn in the outer corners at an angle, using the marks printed on the paper as a guide.

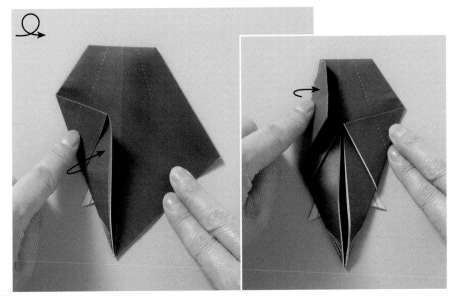

2 Turn the paper over and fold in the lower edges so that they meet along the central crease, then fold in the top edges in the same way.

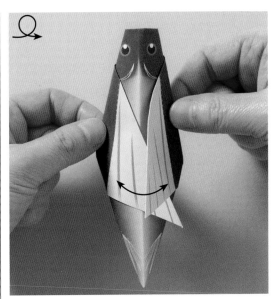

3 Lift up the paper and turn it over, then fold it in half along the central crease, releasing the wings as you finish.

4 Fold back the wings on both sides.

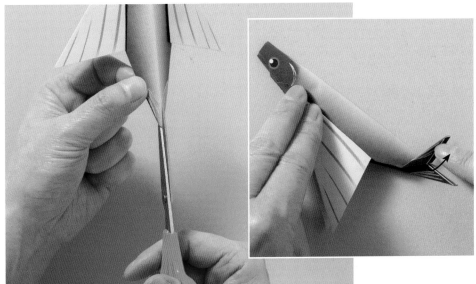

5 Use a pair of scissors to cut along the crease from the right-hand end then turn over the top layer at an angle to form the fish's tail.

32 MAGURO | TUNA

Tuna are big and powerful, their whole body is made of muscle which they use to rip through the strong ocean currents at high speed and swim effortlessly for long distance. The more accurately you can make the model, the more vividly the fish wil reflect its real-life strength!

You will need:
1 sheet of 6in (15cm) origami paper
Scissors

Difficulty rating: ● ○ ○

1 With the design face down, fold the paper in half through the design and open out to form a crease. Turn in the lower edges so that they meet along the crease, then turn the paper over and fold down the top point between the outer points.

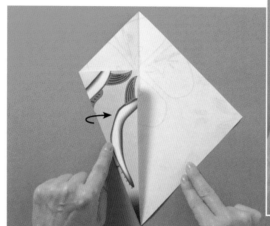

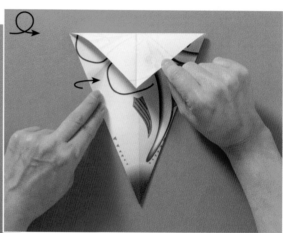

2 Fold over the top corners to make diagonal creases, ensuring that the horizontal edges now meet along the central crease. Turn the paper back over and open out these flaps to form a diamond shape again.

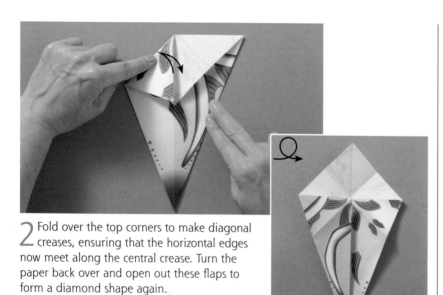

3 Fold over the upper edges along the diagonal crease to reverse their direction and open out again.

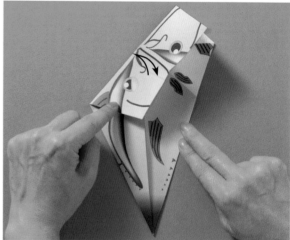

OCEAN INSIGHT

Tuna are a hugely popular fish to eat. In Japan, one tuna was sold for $1.8 million (£1.2 million) to the owner of a chain of sushi restaurants.

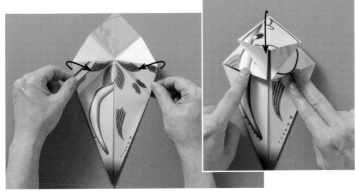

4 Take the outer points and fold them into the center of the model, using the diagonal creases just made. Fold down the top point of the central section into a diamond shape.

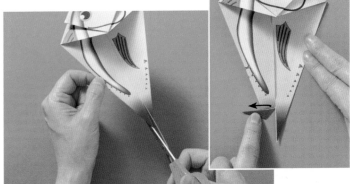

5 Use a pair of scissors to cut along the crease from the right-hand end, then turn over the top layer at an angle to form the fish's tail.

33 UMIGAME | TURTLE

Sea turtles are mysterious creatures who roam the expanses of the ocean, only returning to land to lay their eggs on the very beach on which they were born. Making this origami model of a sea turtle is easy as long as you take care with the basic shape formed in the first step.

You will need:
1 sheet of 6in (15cm) origami paper
Scissors

Difficulty rating: ● ● ○

1 With the design face down, fold the paper in half from corner to corner across the design to make a crease and open out. Fold between the other corners then lift the left-hand point, open out the pocket on the flap, and press forward into a diamond shape. Turn over and repeat.

2 Fold in the lower edges so that they meet along the central crease, then turn the top point down over these flaps to form a crease.

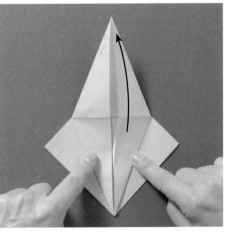

3 Open out the flaps, lifting the bottom point up and over the top to form a diamond shape.

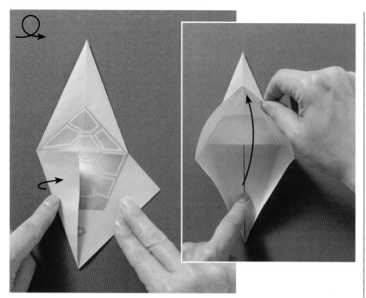

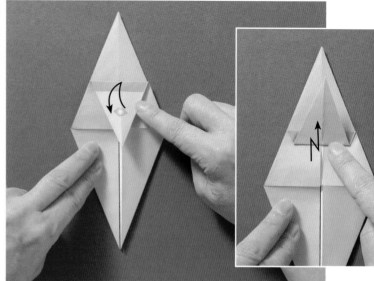

4 Turn the paper over and repeat, first turning in the bottom edges then opening out the flaps and taking the bottom point up to the top point made in the previous step.

5 Fold down the top point, making a horizontal crease at the position indicated by the marks printed on the design, then turn the point back again to form a concertina fold.

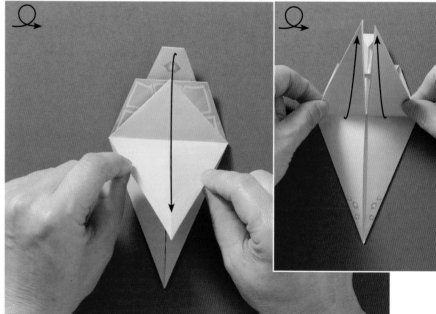

6 Turn the tip back again, also using the marks printed on the design.

7 Turn the paper over and fold the top flap down to the bottom, then turn the paper back over and fold the two flaps from the bottom up to the top.

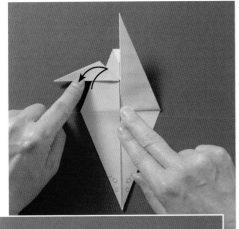

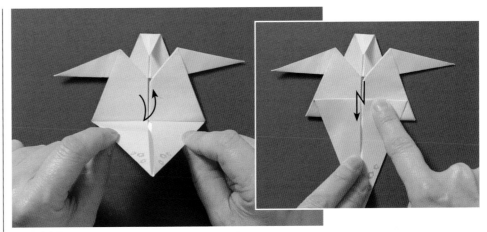

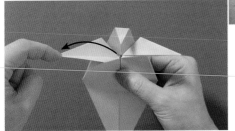

8 Fold the tips of these flaps out to the sides of the model and make diagonal creases, then carefully open up the model and fold the points inside, reversing the direction of the creases as necessary.

9 Fold up the bottom point to make a horizontal crease at the widest part of the model, then turn the tip back down again to form a concertina fold.

10 Pick up the model and use a pair of scissors to cut up the central crease from the right-hand end.

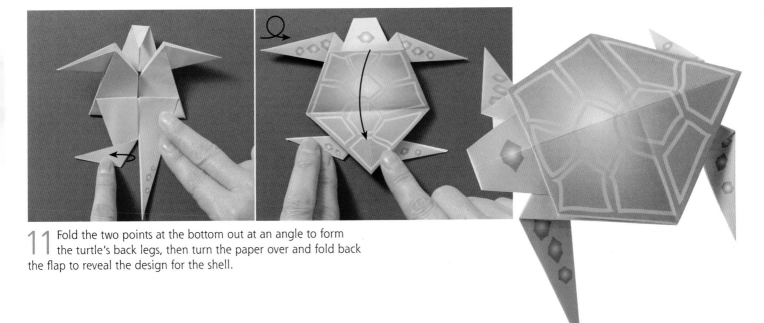

11 Fold the two points at the bottom out at an angle to form the turtle's back legs, then turn the paper over and fold back the flap to reveal the design for the shell.

34 EI | RAY

The ray swims swims through the sea elegantly, gliding for many miles at a time like a huge oceanic kite. That swimming appearance is also popular in the aquarium. This origami model begins with the square-folding technique just used to make the turtle in the previous project. Check the first folds on page 117 if you need a reminder of what to do.

You will need:
1 sheet of 6in (15cm) origami paper

Difficulty rating: ● ● ○

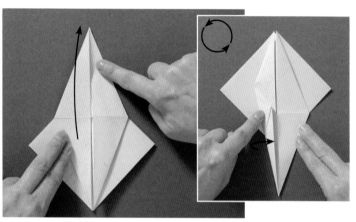

1 Follow steps 1 to 3 of the previous project to reach the position shown in the main image above then spin the paper through 180 degrees and fold in the lower edges of the diamond shape so that they run along the central crease.

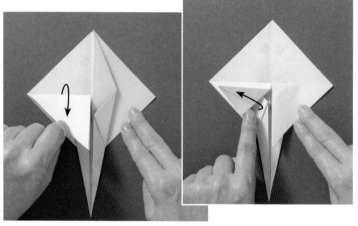

2 Fold down the top points so that two new horizontal creases are formed across the middle of the diamond, then turn back the bottom point of each flap at an angle so that the vertical edge runs across the horizontal fold.

3 Fold the same edges back, this time to the new diagonal folds, then turn back the upper edges of the model at a slight angle from the outer points.

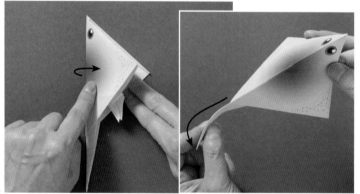

4 Fold the model in half along its length, then carefully bend the ray's tail to give it shape.

OCEAN INSIGHT

The giant oceanic manta ray is the world's biggest ray, with the largest measuring up to 23 feet (7 meters) wide.

35 SUZUKI | JAPANESE BASS

Japanese sea bass live all around the coasts of the country's islands. They only become known as *suzuki*, meaning "excellent fish," when fully grown; when young they are called *seigo*. This origami model has been designed to emphasize the sea bass's characteristic mouth but be careful with the first folds to ensure that the complicated creases are made evenly.

You will need:
1 sheet of 6in (15cm) origami paper

Difficulty rating: ● ● ○

1 With the design face up, fold the paper in half between the corners through the design. Carefully turn the outer corners across each other until you judge that each point exactly sits on what will become the opposite folded edge, then press down firmly.

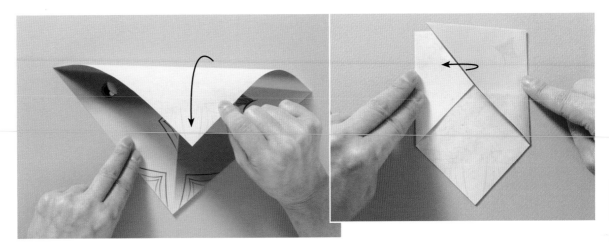

2 Fold both new flaps in half by turning each one's outer point down to the bottom point.

3 Fold the loose tip up from the bottom so that it sits on the top corner of the model, then halve the loose flap again by turning the point down so that the diagonal edge runs horizontally. Repeat on the opposite flap.

4 Turn the paper over and fold the tip of the protruding flap in half. Repeat on the opposite tip.

5 Turn the paper back over, then take the top left corner and make a diagonal crease across the model. Repeat using the top right corner.

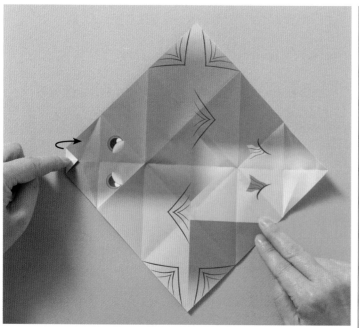

6 Open the paper out, design face up, and turn back the left-hand corner using the closest crease line.

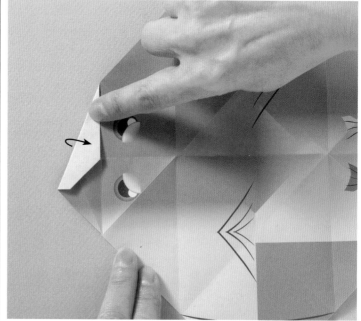

7 Use the nearest diagonal crease to fold back the edge above the left-hand point.

8 Carefully lift up the bottom end of the flap just made, then turn back the edge below the left-hand corner, leaving a small triangular flap standing up in the middle.

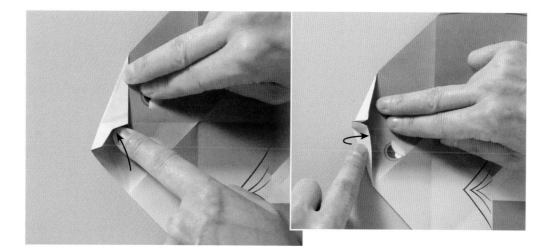

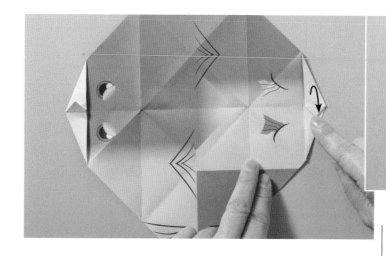

9 Repeat on the right-hand side of the paper, then turn up the bottom point, making a horizontal crease line between the lowest ends of the existing diagonal creases. Repeat on the top.

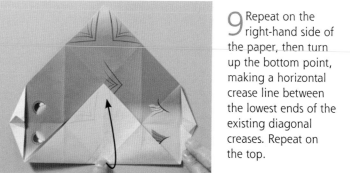

10 Open out and turn the paper over. Fold over each edge in turn, pressing down the crease in the central section.

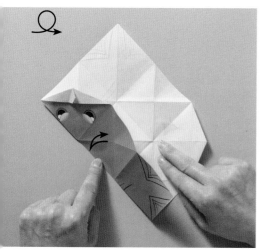

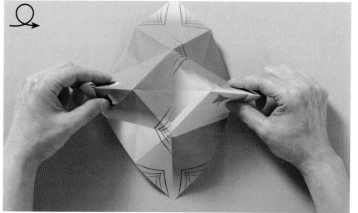

11 Turn the paper back over. Lift the paper up and press the two sides of the left- and right-hand ends together then gently push them downward and toward each other.

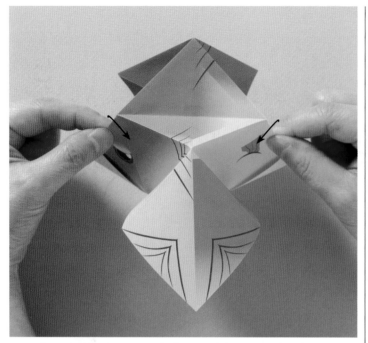

12 As you press the two ends down and in, ensure that the crease across the central section reforms and the top and bottom sides of the central square move together.

13 Put the paper back down on the table and flatten the two flaps into triangles pointing to the right.

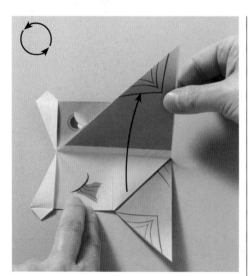

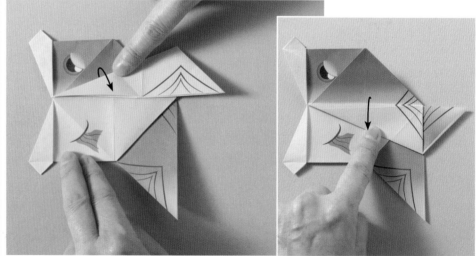

14 Spin the model through 90 degrees and turn the triangular flap up to the top.

15 Fold the flap in half by turning over the diagonal edge so that it runs along the horizontal crease. Fold the flap back down over the same crease.

16 Lift the flap and fold it forward across the vertical crease, then turn up the protruding point across the diagonal edge.

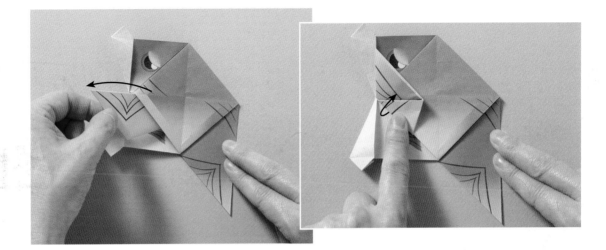

17 Turn the flap back to the right. The top half of the tail has been formed.

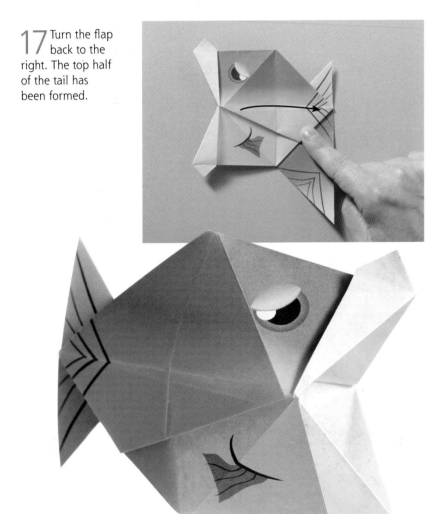

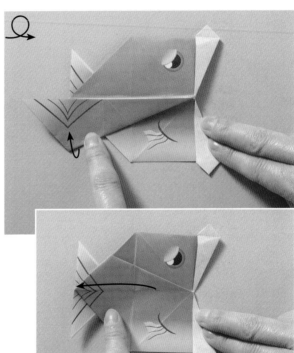

18 Turn the paper over and fold up the diagonal edge of the flap so that it runs along the horizontal crease. Now repeat steps 15–17 to make the second half of the tail.

INDEX

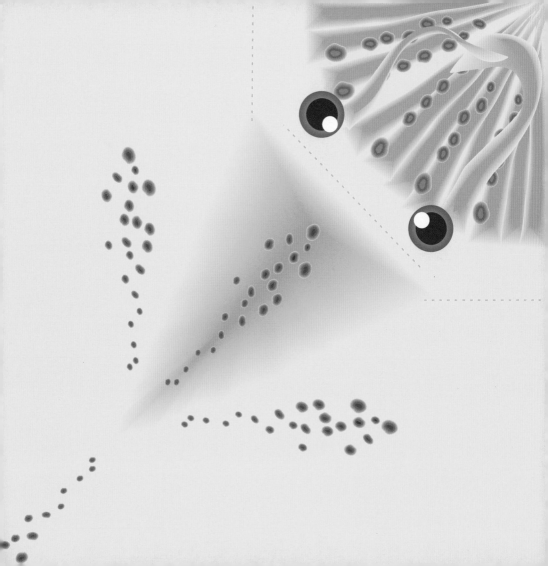

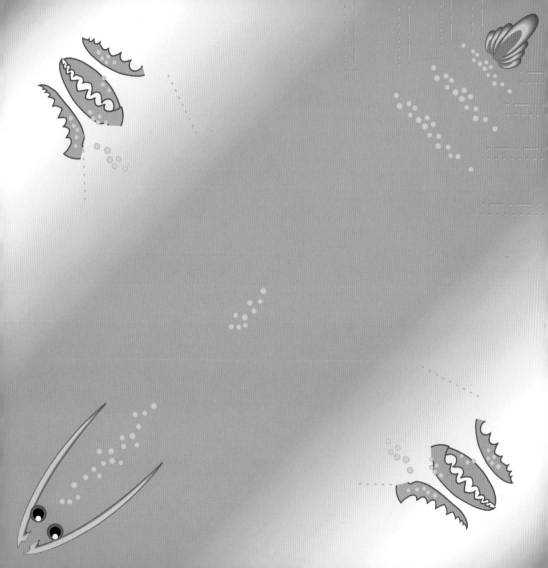

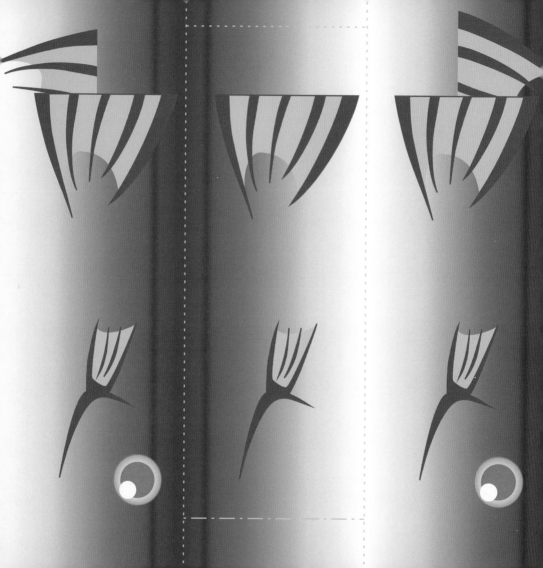

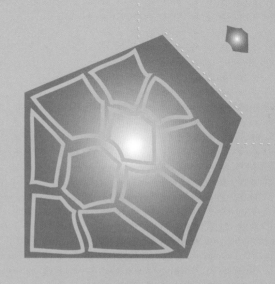

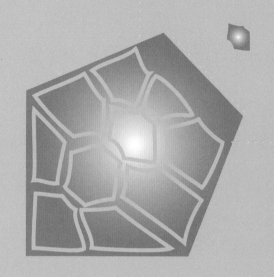

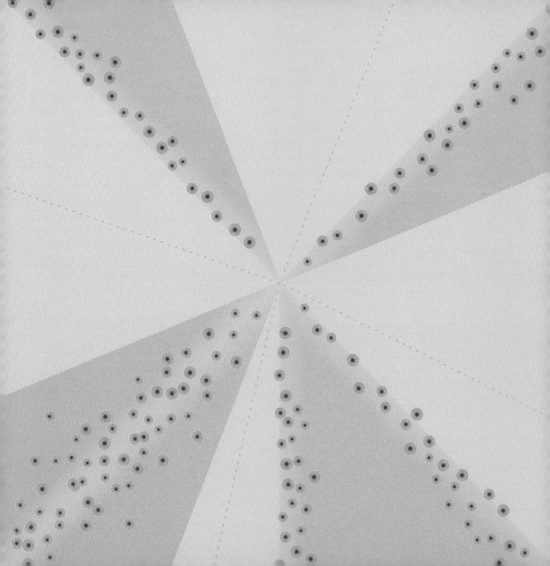

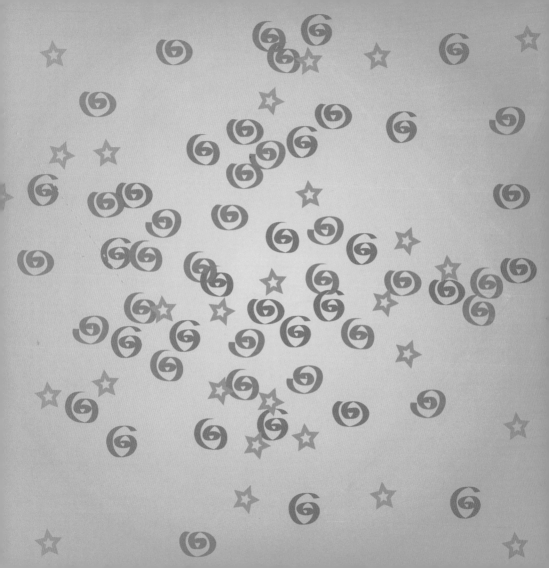

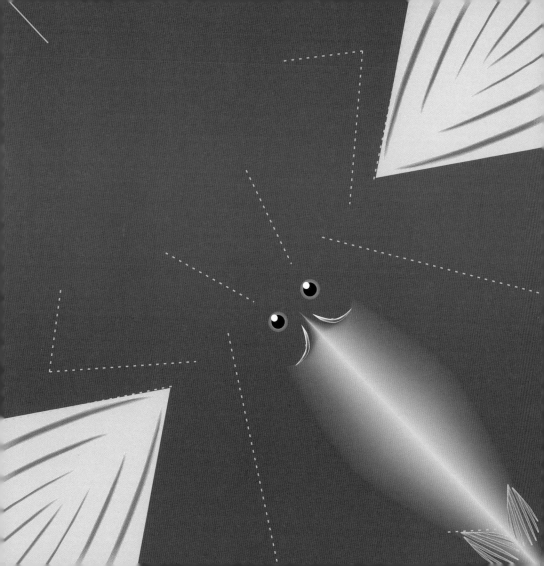

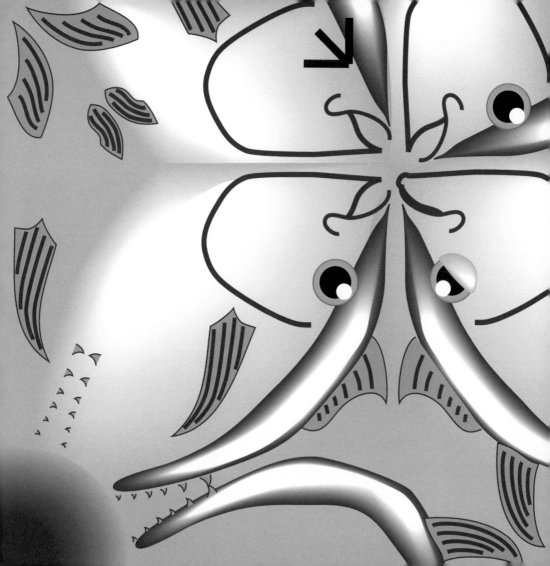

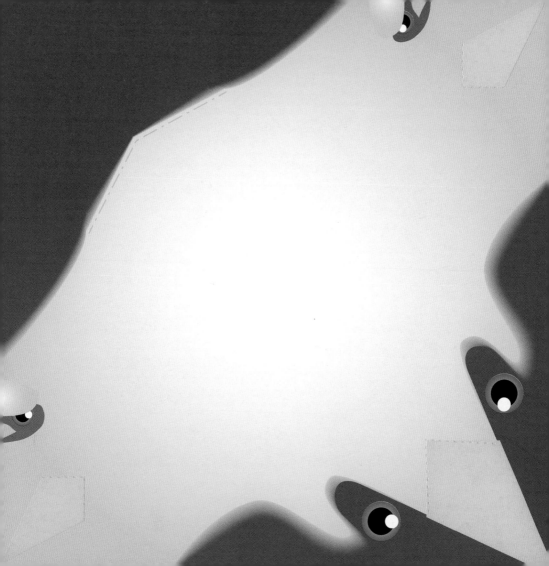

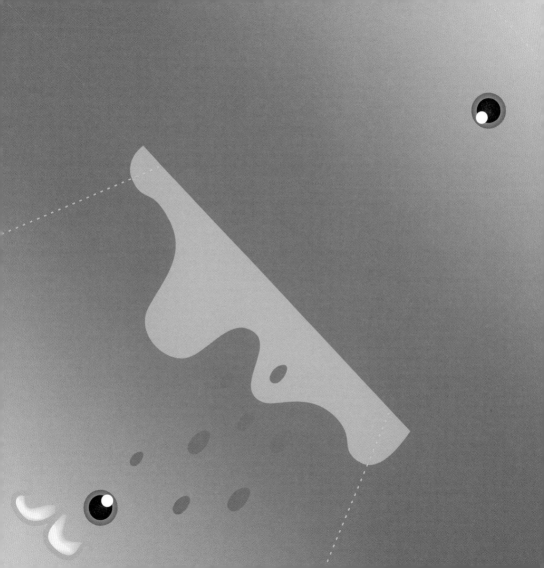

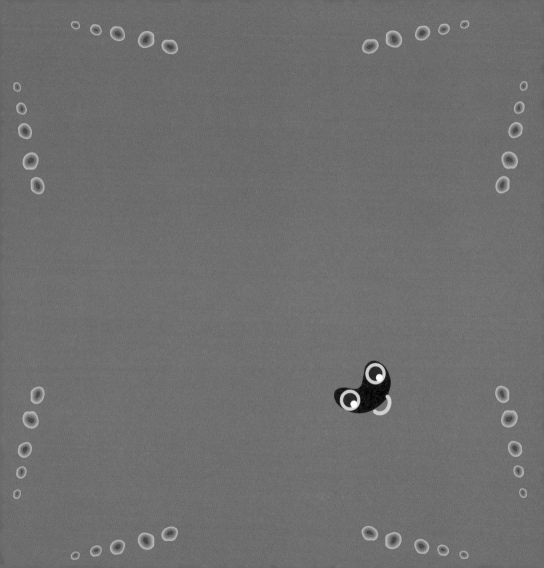